PREMED TO MED

How an ordinary student can find success in
the medical school application process

By Nahee Park

PREMED TO MED
By Nahee Park

*To my parents and siblings for their continuous
support throughout my premed journey*

Cover Art by Camille Sanchez
Follow her at @camipoopedart

© 2019 by Nahee Park
1st edition
ISBN: 9781080805013

CONTENTS

Title Page

Chapter 1: Introduction   1

Chapter 2: Acronym List   5

Chapter 3: Surviving the Premed Weedout   10

Chapter 4: Organizing the Premed Timeline   31

Chapter 5: DO vs MD Application   34

Chapter 6: MCAT® and CASPer® Preparation   42

Chapter 7: What it Means to be an Asian Applicant   62

Chapter 8: Global Medical Missions Trip   72

Chapter 9: Finance   77

Chapter 10: Gap Year   86

Chapter 11: Building your Medical School List   97

Chapter 12: Essay Collections   103

Chapter 13: Recommendation Letter   147

Chapter 14: Interviews   153

Chapter 15: Post Interview Tips   188

Chapter 16: Books to Read   193

Chapter 17: Final Words   195

About the Author   197

References   198

CHAPTER 1:
INTRODUCTION

"Oh, you're taking the easy route," was the response I received from a woman when I told her that I was a pre-med student. I was a sophomore student at Northwestern University waiting for the campus bus to take me to my next class. It was in the middle of winter so I remember I was bundled up in my thick coat, scarf, and a hat to survive the cold Evanston weather. I was hopping up and down in an attempt to warm myself when suddenly a woman behind me, who appeared to be in her 50's tapped me on my shoulder, and asked me what I was studying at Northwestern. I answered that I was majoring in neuroscience and was on the premed track. It was at this moment when the woman smirked and said "Oh, you're taking the easy route." If I was having a good day, I probably would have smiled, laughed, and went along with her. But I guess I was tired that day because I volunteered in the hospital for 4 hours in the morning, took an exam in the afternoon, and was waiting for the bus to take me to my physics lab which would last until 9pm. I guess my facial expression had said it all because she found the need to explain herself, "Well, you're guaranteed a job as long as you stay on the train."

That night, I reflected on what the woman meant by when she said "stay on the train." She was referring that the medical school process was "easy" because I essentially had a structured "to do list' that was straight forward. All pre-med students know that they should complete all pre-med courses, take the MCAT & Casper test, gain clinical experience, volunteer, shadow physicians, and perform research. What she meant was that while other non-premed students were finishing school and applying to jobs without direction or guarantee, the premed students "just" had to complete a "list of to do items" to get in the medical school which would pretty much guarantee a job in the healthcare world.

If my brain was working faster during my encounter with her, perhaps I would have said that it was difficult hopping on the train and holding onto the train. That being said, I also agree with what she said because premeds know exactly what they have to do before applying to medical school in terms of what classes to enroll, what exams to take, what kind of volunteering to do, etc. Of course, our motivation and passion for medicine has to be present. However, I guess being premed is the "easy route" because we have "How to get into medical school" resources available, while there are no such resources that explain "How to get hired at XXX company."

In more seriousness, welcome to the guide of a pre-med life. If you have picked up this book, I assume that you are either a student interested in medicine, or the parent of a child who is preparing to become a physician. Unlike many other professions where only a bachelor's degree is required, I understand that becoming a physician is not something that you one day "decision to take upon." To put it into perspective, applying to medical school as a competitive applicant requires a solid GPA & MCAT score, research experience, clinical experience, community service, letter of recommendation, leadership activities, extra-curricular involvement, primary application, and secondary application. Medical schools are now implementing more requirements such as the new personality test CASPer®. I'm already overwhelmed by listing all the factors that are involved in the medical school admissions process. This exhaustive process will truly differentiate students who are serious and committed to medicine, and those who are really unsure of their path of becoming a physician. As you can imagine, the process of a medical school acceptance is an extremely long journey. In order to prepare all the qualifications joyfully, you will have to have a natural compassion to serve people in need and have a passion in the medical field. Additionally, arming yourself with the knowledge of the entire application process will be a valuable asset through your medical school journey.

Whether you are a student or parent, I believe that this book will be a great starting point to understand the life of a premed student and the steps you should take for a successful medical school application journey. Since this book shares my personal journey of the application process, please keep in mind that I am only 1 data point and that my story is only one of many successfully stories out there; however, I hope that my story and advices will serve as a powerful guide to your medical school application journey.

The second reason why I am writing this book is to show you that it is possible to get into medical school as an ordinary applicant. Strictly speaking, I believe that my academic scores lay around 60th – 75th percentile of all medical school applicants. All too many times, I have read books or articles from admissions officers or counseling coaches that share how they were able to support their student to "go to Harvard." After reading their stories, I was often discouraged to find out that the Harvard applicant had scored a 525 on their MCAT, published a renowned research study, or was armed with an incredible personal narrative that was unheard of. While these books share great successful stories of qualified, deserving applicants, I believe that these inflated stories are not extremely helpful for ordinary hard working students. Therefore, I hope to share how I, an ordinary applicant, was able to receive multiple medical school acceptances.

Third, I believe that my book is different from any other "How to get into Medical School" books because I am neither an admissions officer, nor a medical school counselor, nor a physician. However, I believe that my story is unique and powerful because I recently finished the application cycle and can offer perspective and personal advices that an admissions officer will not be able to provide. Throughout my story, I share my personal experiences, obstacles, and lessons that I have learned from the past 4-5 years of being a pre-med student. I also offer advices that are differentiated with the symbol ♠ so you can learn from my mistakes and avoid doing the same thing.

With that being said, hop on the train, and let's take a ride!

CHAPTER 2:
ACRONYM LIST

There are a list of acronyms and vocabs you will come across as you begin to understand the medical school application process. I attempt to write out the full name of the abbreviations throughout my book as I introduce them to you; however, I created the Acronym List so you can revert back to this page when you are confused about a certain Acronym. I also provide a quick definition of each terms below in alphabetical order.

AAMC®: Association of American Medical Colleges®
This organization runs the AMCAS and MCAT, and represents allopathic medical schools.

AACOM®: The American Association of College of Osteopathic Medicine®
This organization runs the AACOMAS, and represents osteopathic medical schools.

AACOMAS®: American Association of Colleges of Osteopathic Medicine Application Service
This is known as the common application system when applying to osteopathic medical schools.

ACGME®: The Accreditation Council for Graduate Medical Education
The members of the ACGME will review and accredit residencies and fellowships.

Allopathic Medical Schools

This is the traditional medical system that most people are familiar with. Students graduating from allopathic medical schools will receive the M.D. degree.

AMCAS®: The American Medical College Application Service
This is known as the common application system when applying to allopathic medical schools.

AP: Advanced Placement
Exam taken during high school that allows students to gain college credit

CASPer®: Computer-Based Assessment for Sampling Personal Characteristics
An admission test that measures subjective characteristics such as communication, empathy, ethics, and professionalism

COCA®: Commission on Osteopathic College Accreditation
Members of the CCOA will review and accredit osteopathic medical schools.

COMLEX®: Comprehensive Medical Licensing Examination
Osteopathic students must complete the Complex exams in order to receive the practicing license.

D.O: Doctor of Osteopathic Medicine
Students graduating from Osteopathic Medical Schools will receive a D.O degree.

EFC: Effective Family Contribution
EFC is the realistic amount that the student's family or parents are willing to contribute to the student's college expense. EFC will be considered in the overall financial loans.

FAFSA®: The Free Application for Federal Student Aid
A financial form applied to receive federal aid including loans, work-study opportunities, and grants.

FAP®: Fee Assistance Program

Run by AAMC, students eligible for FAP will receive financial assistance such has free MCAT exam & free medical school applications.

GPA: Grade Point Average
A method of measuring academic achievement during the undergraduate career
cGPA: cumulative grade point average (total GPA earned in college)
sGPA: science grade point average (GPA only measured from science courses)

LCME®: Liaison Committee on Medical Education
Members of the LCME will review and accredit allopathic medical schools.

LOR: Letter of Recommendation
Medical schools will require students to submit recommendation letters from professors, advisers, research mentors, etc.

MCAT®: The Medical College Admission Test
A standardized entrance exam that must be complete before applying to medical school
There are 4 sections that comprise the exam:
Chem/Phys: Chemical and Physical Foundations of Biological Systems
CARS: Critical Analysis and Reasoning Skills
Bio/Biochem: Biological and Biochemical Foundations of Living Systems
Psych/Soc: Psychological, Social, and Biological Foundations of Behavior

M.D.: Medical Degree
Students graduating from Allopathic Medical Schools will receive a M.D degree.

MS: Medical Student

MSAR®: The Medical School Admissions Requirements
Online database from AAMC that allows students to search information of all allopathic medical schools

OMM: Osteopathic Manipulative Medicine
This curriculum is taught to students in osteopathic medical schools. Students learn how to make noninvasive skeletal adjustments to realign with the natural body.

OOS: Out of State
Out of state students are applicants who are applying to a medical school that is not located in their state of permanent residence. There may be several pros and cons to being a OOS student for each medical school.

ORM: Over-represented in Medicine

Osteopathic Medical Schools
Students in Osteopathic medical schools receive training in manipulation. Graduation from an Osteopathic medical school will grant a D.O degree.

PR: Princeton Review
A third party college admission service company that offers test preparation services, consulting, admissions resources, and interview preparation services.

Secondary Application
After a primary application has been sent through the AMCAS, schools will decide whether to give a secondary application invitation to students. Secondary applications will include essay questions to understand more about the applicant.

USMLE®: United States Medical Licensing Exam
Allopathic students must pass 3 USMLE step exams in order to receive their practicing license

W&A: Work and Activities
A section of the primary application that allows students to list

and explain all previous experiences

WL: Waitlist

After interviewing, students may be placed in a waitlist. This decision is neither an acceptance nor a rejection. A student in waitlist may be accepted a seat was withdrawn by an accepted student.

CHAPTER 3:
SURVIVING THE
PREMED WEEDOUT

You finally leaped over the first hurdle of being accepted to an undergraduate institution and thought you were one step closer to becoming a physician. You were excited to attend your first college class and walked into a 300 seat Chemistry lecture room. Let me guess, you were also instantly overwhelmed by the number of students who raised their hand after the professor asked "How many of you guys are premed?" I'm sure the next statement that was made by your professor was to "run away while you could."

I remember attending my first chemistry course and was surprised to see an exhausting number of premed students. The professor announced to the crowd of 150 students that half the students would be "weeded out." Of course, all the pre-med students, including me, were probably thinking that it was certainly not us who would be weeded out. You are probably aware of the term "weeding out." Whether colleges weed out students directly or indirectly, all colleges will weed out premed students. Meaning, the number of premed students will drop substantially every semester because they could not pass the class, give up after taking a few classes, or decide to pursue another wanted career.

Colleges will weed students out for numerous reasons:

Colleges want to increase their "medical school matriculation percentage."
The only way to do this is to weed out students so that only competitive students will even think about applying to medical school. For example, Northwestern Pre-health advisers state that 75% of students with a GPA of 3.5 will be accepted to at least 1 medical school[1]. Of course, these 75% of students are not referring to the freshman pre-med students, but rather, this is referring to the number of students who survived through the weeding out process, completed the MCAT, and were applying to medical school. Therefore, be cautious when you hear admission officers advertising how well they send students to medical school.

On a more humanistic level, colleges want to ensure that students are prepared and also have the passion to attend medical school.
I have many friends who were premed either because their parents wanted them to be premed, or they were unsure what other opportunities were available. A weeding out process will allow these students to realize the path of becoming a physician is not for them.

If you are a student who is compassionate, dedicated to medicine, and believe that this is the right profession for you, then your initial goal as a freshman and sophomore student is to survive the weed out process. In my opinion, sustaining a minimum GPA of 3.7 will be crucial to be a competitive medical school applicant.

Premed Requirements

There are premed course requirements that you will need successfully complete before matriculating into medical school. Are you taking appropriate courses? Are you taking advanced coursework? The key to planning your course schedule is to proactively seek information and understand admission requirements. By visiting MSAR (Medical School Admission Requirements) or the Osteopathic Medical College Information Booklet, you can see the detailed course requirements of each school. I advise you to update yourself on all the necessary prerequisite information to avoid any delays or setbacks in the future. It is recommended to complete these prerequisite courses prior to applying to medical schools as evidence that you are competent in these basic courses. Additionally, completing these courses prior to taking the MCAT will ensure that you develop a strong foundation to do well on the test.

The basic pre-med requirements will normally include the following[2]:

General Chemistry (1 year + lab)
Organic Chemistry (1 year + lab)
Biology (1 year + lab)
Biochemistry (1 course)
Physics (1 year + lab)
Math (2 semesters calculus + 1 statistics course)
English (1 year)
Behavioral and Social Sciences (1 year)

♠ Most medical schools will accept AP credit, but some may require or recommend you to take upper level coursework. There are also numerous medical schools that do not accept AP or IB credits. Additionally, not all medical schools have the same requirements. Therefore, buy the MSAR resource from the AAMC website to know school-specific requirements. It would be a shame to not be able to apply to your dream schools just because you did not fulfill their course requirements!

Choosing your Major

Choosing a major may be one of your most important decision to make as an undergraduate student. While many pre-med advisers will say that you can pursue any major as a pre-med student, I believe that some majors are better than others. As always, "pre-med" is not a major.

Will a certain major look better to medical school admissions?
It is generally assumed that your major will not play a huge factor in influencing the admission's decision. While students will recognize that some majors will be more difficult than others, you should not expect to be compensated for a lower GPA because your major is "harder." Always keep in mind that your major will not matter as much as your GPA. I encourage students to choose a major that interests them, and that they can do well in, rather than choosing a major to put it on the resume.

Majoring in a unique major such as theatrical arts, philosophy, or architecture may be interesting to the admissions officers and also would be an interesting topic to talk about during your interviews. However, these majors will not necessary put you at an advantage. In addition, if you decide to major in something unique, be prepared to answer the interview question, "Why did you decide to major in XXX?," especially if it has nothing to do with your passion in medicine.

What is the most common pre-med major?
Biology is by far, the most common pre-med major. It is not surprising that many students choose to major in biology considering that it is the main basis of medical principles; however, more students are starting to major in non-science majors such as psychology, sociology, math, or even engineering.

Some students believe that majoring in biology will help prepare them for the MCAT. However, AAMC performed a study called "MCAT and GPAs for Applicants and Matriculants to U.S. Medical Schools by Primary Undergraduate Major 2018-2019" which displayed that students who majored in biology did not necessarily perform better on the biological section of the MCAT[3]. In fact, there was not a statistically significant correlation between a student's undergraduate major and his/her performance on any section in the MCAT. The following graphs taken from the AAMC data collection display the MCAT section scores of students who were **accepted** to medical school.

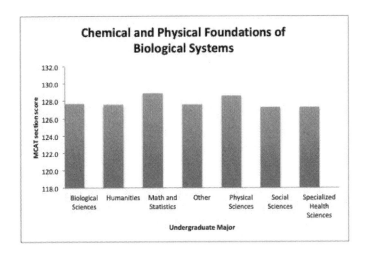

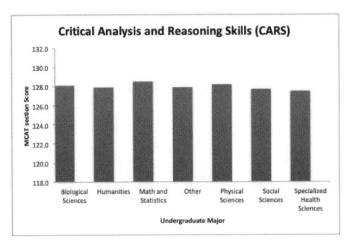

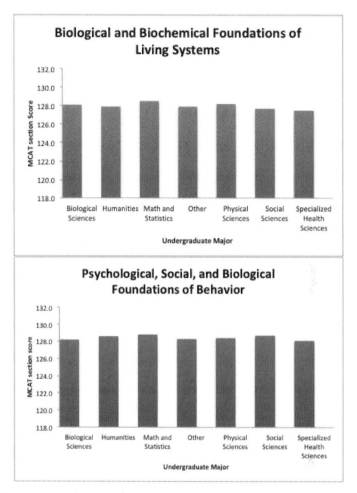

(Adapted from: AAMC Table A-17: MCAT and GPAs for Applicants and Matriculants to U.S. Medical Schools by Primary Undergraduate Major, 2018) www.aamc.org/download/321496/data/factstablea17.pdf

Therefore, I encourage you to look into other majors especially if you have other interests. I majored in neuroscience because I have always been interested in cognition, sleep, and behaviors. I thought my classes were far more interesting than my friend's biology classes, so I enjoyed every single class! While choosing a major will not impact your MCAT score or a medical school admissions, I am most certain that choosing a major of your interest will boost your GPA since you will have an internal motivation to study harder and attend office hours.

What is the difference between cumulative GPA and science GPA?
There are two different types of GPA (cumulative GPA and science GPA) that will be calculated in your application. Cumulative GPA (cGPA) is the overall GPA based on all courses taken throughout the student's college career. Science GPA (sGPA) represents the GPA based on only a select number of courses. The science GPA for allopathic programs include all courses in chemistry, biology, neuroscience, physics, and math. The science GPA for osteopathic programs include all courses in biology, chemistry, neuroscience, and physics only. Therefore, it is important to do well in your science courses as well as your non-science courses.

Thoughts on selecting a non-science major?
I believe that majoring in a non-science is beginning to gain popularity. While I discussed that there is no one major that will help students get into medical school, I believe that selecting a non-science major allows the admissions officers to understand that you are a well-rounded student, of course, only if he/she can excel on their MCAT and science pre-requisite courses. This is likely due to admissions reviewing an applicant's application in a holistic manner. However, there a few things to know before deciding on a non-science major. First of all, make sure you are aware of the basic prerequisite classes for medical schools. You may need to make extra room in your schedule to take requirements for your major as well as complete the medical school prerequisites. In order to graduate on time, you may need to take classes during the summer or take more academic courses than the average student. This is why I personally respect pre-med students who are music majors or dance majors. I think it's incredible for them to fulfill their major courses, attend rehearsals, put on performances, as well as completing all pre-med prerequisites.

Why do I recommend students to major in sciences?

Personally speaking, I believe majoring in sciences is easier for pre-med students for two reasons. First, as a science major, taking science courses will not only fulfill your science major requirements, but it will also fulfill the pre-med requirements at the same time. Talk about killing two birds with one stone! Since one course is fulfilling multiple requirements, it is easier to graduate on time, or even earlier.

Second, a student majoring in sciences will likely have a better science GPA than a student majoring in a non-science. Due to the rigors of the pre-med prerequisites which includes chemistry, biology, organic chemistry, biochemistry, and physics, a student's freshman and sophomore science GPA will likely be low. Luckily, I found that my junior and senior science courses were much easier to get an A (because the weeding out process was over). Since I maintained a 4.0 during all my junior and senior classes, this significantly increased my overall science and cumulative GPA. If a student majors in non-sciences, then they will most likely not take additional science courses during their junior and senior year. If they did poorly in their premed prerequisite class during their freshman and sophomore year, then they will have fewer opportunities to raise their science GPA compared to a student who is majoring in a science field.

Surviving the Premed Track

Premed Curriculum Advice

My personal advice to you is to take all the premed courses at your undergraduate institution rather than using AP or IB credit to test out of introductory courses. Although you may have received a 5 on your AP exam which gives you the option of testing out of courses, I believe it is beneficial to take the college premed courses. For the purposes of clarity, I will provide a specific example. At Northwestern University, two different levels of chemistry (a pre-med prerequisite) is offered: introductory Chemistry and Advanced Chemistry. Students who do not place out of chemistry will take introductory Chemistry which lasts 3 quarters. Students who received a 3 or higher on the chemistry AP exam can choose to take Advanced Chemistry which is only 2 quarters. Students who received a 5 on the chemistry AP exam can place out of the entire chemistry sequence and jump right into Organic Chemistry. Let's go through each of the scenario in more detail:

Student Group A takes Introductory Chemistry
Student group A consists of students who either did not take the chemistry AP exam, did not score high enough on the Chemistry AP exam, or decided to take Introductory Chemistry despite scoring high on the AP exam. Since Introductory Chemistry is 3 quarters long and easier than the advanced chemistry course, this gives students the possibility to receive 3 A's that will be added to the science GPA.

Student Group B takes Advanced Chemistry
Student group B consists of students who took the Chem AP and received a 3 or higher. Since Advanced Chemistry is only 2 quarters, students who do well can receive 2 A's. However, since Advanced Chemistry is more difficult than Introductory Chemistry, students will have to work harder to receive an A in the course.

Student Group C places out of Inorganic Chemistry and takes Organic Chemistry
Student group C consists only of students who received a 5 on the chemistry AP exam. They decided to place out of Inorganic Chemistry and jump straight into organic chemistry either as a freshman or sophomore student. Some students will own it and do well. However, for the majority of students, I believe that the decision to place out of Inorganic Chemistry and go straight to Organic Chemistry is a wrong choice.

1. For the purposes of maintaining a high GPA, a student needs as many A's as they can get.
   If a student received a score of 5 on the chemistry AP exam, this means they have a very strong understanding

of inorganic chemistry. If students decide to place out of Inorganic Chemistry using their AP credit, then they do not have the opportunity to "collect A's" from the Inorganic Chemistry courses. Although these students are not guaranteed to receive an "A' in inorganic chemistry, I believe that they are likely to receive A's in Inorganic Chemistry because they were able to score a 5 on the chemistry AP exam. Taking organic chemistry right off the bat means that student group C will most likely take upper level chemistry courses in which it is no longer "an easy A."

Disclaimer: I believe that students should challenge themselves and take difficult courses to enhance their knowledge and deepen their critical thinking skills. We shouldn't waste neither our college time nor tuition money by taking easy courses. However, I provide this example purely from the perspective of what we can do in order to maintain a high GPA.

2. Students who immediately take organic chemistry are more prone to do poorly. Although student group C did well in the chemistry AP exam, I promise you that college chemistry is more difficult than the chemistry AP exam. Student group A and B have already experienced the rigors of college chemistry and thus, are more prone to do better than student group C in organic chemistry. Many students who decide to take Organic Chemistry during their freshman year drop out and end up retaking this course during their sophomore year. Therefore, I encourage students to take Inorganic Chemistry at your undergraduate institution prior to taking Organic Chemistry.

♠ I am sharing this personal analysis to show that students who come to college with numerous AP tests and place out of numerous courses are not necessarily at an advantage when applying to medical school. While some students take harder courses to "show admission officers that they can handle rigorous courses," this only works if they do well in those courses. If you continuously receive a B or C in rigorous courses, this will impact you more negatively. In my example, I was very strategic with having the best GPA. Although I was told numerous times that my grades were not the end all be all, I have to tell you, GPA is extremely important and it will truly define you as a candidate. Therefore, while taking rigorous courses is important, receiving a higher GPA is more important. At the same time, I wanted to be academically challenged. Therefore, I decided to take "Advanced Chemistry" rather than Introductory Chemistry.

According to the Northwestern Health Professions Advising office, the acceptance rate by science GPA for first-time Northwestern applicants in 2017 is shown in the table below[1]. Please keep in mind that these numbers are students who survived the weeding out process, took the MCAT, and were certain that they wanted to pursue a career in medicine.

sGPA > 3.2: 75%	sGPA > 3.4: 80%	sGPA > 3.6: 88%	sGPA> 3.8: 100%

Applying to Medical School. Northwestern University HPA. (n.d.)

Now, I don't know about you, but I see a clear correlation here. Although medical schools are now emphasizing their "holistic application" process where GPA is only a part of the factor, I encourage you to maintain at least a 3.7 GPA by the time you apply to medical school. In order to maintain a good GPA, you will have to be smart about what courses you choose and when you take those courses. I personally took all my premed classes as a freshman and sophomore in college and didn't do so well on my premed courses. Now looking back, I wish I had spread them out.

Studying Behaviors
A fun fact about me is that I have never pulled an all-nighter, and

I do not plan on ever pulling an all-nighter. Honestly, this fact should not be a shocker because it is not necessary (especially in college). My advice is to stay organized and don't procrastinate. Stay on top of your homework including problem sets, lab reports, and daily readings. If you see that you are either falling behind, or having difficulty understanding material, get help. Most schools have free tutoring programs that can provide resources and individual teaching time. Attend TA (teaching assistant) or professor's office hours. They are supplying free time for you, and you need to take advantage of it.

However, if you find yourself truly struggling in a course, it might be worth dropping the course if it is before the drop-deadline. If you decide to drop a course after the drop deadline, this will result a "withdrawal" in your course transcript which is the worst option (unless you have a legitimate reason to withdraw a course). Be studious and attend office hours! Who knows, you might be needing to ask them for a letter of recommendation later.

Have Fun

Don't forget to have fun. I'm sure there will be hundreds of fun electives to take while in college. Even though you are probably stressing about your chemistry course, I encourage you to take electives you are genuinely interested in. This will make studying a lot easier and make your premed track a little more exciting. Some unique courses that I decided to take was Russian literature (which was deemed a "must take" course at Northwestern University), Korean Diaspora, New Testament, Buddhist Psychology, and Social Psychology. If I did not graduate early, I would have wanted to take classes in acting, drawing, or ceramics. Even though I said that your GPA matters, don't let this prevent you from taking challenging classes that you're interested in. Also, try not to take too many "blow off" classes where you won't be learning anything. Think about it this way, you are paying expensive tuition. Why waste it on "astronomy

101" when you can be taking a much harder course with more output? Find new horizons you didn't even knew existed and enjoy your college years. It's going to fly and might as well enjoy it.

Possible Plan B

It is normal for any premed student to question if they should pursue medicine. Whether you are confident about your path to medicine or not, it is smart to have a Plan B in case your original plan is interrupted. This doesn't mean that you need to double major in another field. Although, students who are premed and also majoring in engineering or economics will have a more straightforward Plan B. Unfortunately, if you are a student who is majoring in the sciences and don't want to do research as your future career, identifying a Plan B can be trickier.

♠ When I was a sophomore student, I started to freak out about my MCAT and was wondering what I could do with my life if I didn't score well on the test. Since I was a neuroscience major, I knew that performing research would have been an option; however, I knew that I did not want to do research for the rest of my life. Therefore, I looked into other healthcare options such as pharmacy or dentistry. To understand the daily work of a pharmacist, I decided to shadow pharmacists and learned more about pharmacy school. This process was especially important for me because I realized that pharmacy wasn't for me. I also knew that dentistry wasn't something I particularly wanted to do. Luckily, the more I learned about other healthcare options, the more I wanted to pursue medicine. Therefore, my plan B was to also apply to Osteopathic medicine schools due to their lower MCAT average scores. My plan C was to become a physician assistant if I was rejected from allopathic (MD) and osteopathic (DO) medical schools.

Extracurricular Activities/
Resume Building

Before I discuss the different components in a medical school application, I believe it's important to discuss "the checklist." As I have discussed before, many students believe that they can be a competitive candidate if they fulfill requirements in research, clinical volunteer, community service, teaching assistant, etc. While having these experiences under your belt will pose as a great advantage compared to applicants who were not involved in these activities, premed students will sometimes pursue opportunities merely to buff up their medical school resumes. However, if you pursue an extracurricular activity that you do not have interest in, this time spent will not only be miserable and stressful to you, but admissions officers will know that you were just trying to check the boxes. More specifically, even though you are involved in an impressive opportunity, if you are not able to relay that experience in a way that demonstrates your passion and your motivation to pursue medicine, then it's not going to be as impressive as you think it will be. Medical school admissions officers review thousands of applicants each year which means they will know how to differentiate candidates who are genuine and those who are not.

On the other hand, most proactive pre-med students will have many extra-curricular activities they will want to participate in. The key to balancing academics with extra-curricular activities is to limit yourself.

♠ When I was in high school, I wanted to immerse in every extra-curricular activity I was interested in. I refused to limit myself in the number of activities because I didn't want to miss out on a cool experience. Therefore, I involved myself in over 10 different extra-curricular activities as a high school student. Even though I was heavily involved in about 5 activities, I believe that I spread myself too thin for the rest of the clubs. Therefore, as an undergraduate student, I decided to limit myself on the quantity of clubs and increase my participation and leadership instead.

♠ As a general rule of thumb, it is best to immerse in diverse types of activities to become a well-rounded applicant. I divided each activity that you can participate in college in terms of "Required, Highly recommend, and generally recommend."

Required	Highly Recommend	Generally Recommend
Research	Leadership position in Medical-based Club	Leadership position in Non-Medical-based Club
Clinical Experience	Teaching Assistant/ Mentor/Tutor	Sports (Varsity, IM, club) or Music
Physician Shadowing	Community Service	

With that being said, I list a couple of noteworthy experiences and opportunities that you should think about doing during your college experience. Do not feel compelled to accomplish all the activities that I mention below. Remember, it is best to participate in an activity for a longer period of time than to do multiple short-term events.

EDUCATION/ACADEMICS
- Highschool/College - Major/Minor
- Cumulative GPA & Science GPA
- MCAT Test Scores
- Study Abroad
- Teaching Assistant Positions

AWARDS
- Research Grant
- Scholarship awards
- Merit based awards

RESEARCH (Paid, Unpaid)
- Research Projects
- Research Oral or Poster Presentation
- Publications

LEADERSHIP EXPERIENCES
- Extra-curricular Activities (during college)

- Programs (outside college)
- Employment

NON-LEADERSHIP EXTRA-CURRICULUAR ACTIVITIES
- Sport Clubs
- Tutoring/Mentoring

SERVICE OUTREACH
- Extra-curricular Activities that are community service-based
- Long Term outreach
- Church
- Philanthropic events in Sorority or Fraternity
- International medical missions trip (attend more than once)

CLINICAL EXPERIENCES (Unpaid)
- Shadowing Experiences (50-100 hours of various specialties)
- Hospital Volunteer (50-100 hours of various departments)
- Certifications (EMT-B, technician)

CLINICAL EXPERIENCES (Paid)
- Medical Scribe, EMT-B, technician, phlebotomy)

MISCELLANEOUS
- Language Fluency
- Musical Talents
- Cool certifications
- Military Service
- Hobbies

I have attached my resume to give you a glimpse of the activities that I was involved during college and during my gap year.

NAHEE PARK RESUME

EDUCATION

Northwestern University/ BA in Neuroscience:
cGPA: 3.71/4.0 sGPA 3.70/4.0 Class of 2018
Illinois Mathematics and Science Academy:
3.8/4.0 Class of 2014

RESEARCH/Teaching Assistant

Molecular Genetics of Sleep and Circadian Rhythm at Northwestern University Dr. Allada's Neurobiology Lab [10 hours/week]	2016- 2017

My two independent research projects focused on the circadian and homeostatic regulation of the sleep-wake cycle in mice and *Drosophila* flies respectively.

Role and pathway of non-specific cationic channel (NALCN) in Mammalian Circadian Rhythm using mice
Aimed to answer how the knockdown of NALCN affects sleeping behavior, how the molecular clock transcript affects membrane activity via ion channels, and if NALCN can regulate the molecular clock.

To Test Whether Manipulating Synapse Formation in the Brain Alters Sleep Drive in Drosophila
To identify the location of known modulators of sleep homeostasis and how it modulates rebound sleep after sleep deprivation.
Lab experiences: mouse and *Drosophila* genetics, animal behavior, pcr, gel electrophoresis.
Awarded Academic Year Undergraduate Research Grant and Weinberg Summer Research Grant Awards

Health Psychology Northwestern Research [20 hours/week]	Spring 2016-Summer 2016

Identifying how socioeconomic status affects Asthma or cardiovascular diseases in adolescents.
Lab experiences include culturing and harvesting blood samples, analyzing blood data, and conducting dry lab tasks such as

data entry and calling participants for post-clinic surveys. Awarded Summer Internship Program Grant

Northshore Research Center Internship [8 hrs/week, 26 weeks/year]	2012-Winter 2014

Physical Interactions of Regulatory Sequences within Schizophrenia Associated MIR 137 Locus

Examined which genes among MIR137, MIR2682, or other adjacent genes are regulated by regulatory sequences at the Schizophrenia associated MIR137 locus

Northwestern Biology Lab Teaching Assistant [2 quarters]	Spring 2017, Fall 2017

– Genetic and Molecular Processes Lab, Investigative Lab
– Assisted undergraduate students in laboratory techniques and experiments in fundamental aspects of biology.

WORK ACTIVITIES

Emergency Department Physician Scribe (Full-Time)	Winter 2018-April 2019

– Performed documentation and other non-clinical tasks on behalf of the ER physician & mid-level providers

LanguageWill Biology & Chemistry AP and SAT subject Tutor (Part-Time)	Winter 2018-May 2019

– Tutored Biology and Chemistry standardized tests to South Korean students who are planning to attend a college in the United States. All sessions are in Korean/English and performed via video chat.

VOLUNTEER

Medlife Cusco, Peru Summer Brigade Trip [9hours/5days]	June 24th – July 2nd 2017

– Set up Mobile Clinics, assisted physicians and dentists with procedures, gathered medication under the supervision of pharmacists, applied fluoride to children, educated children

and families of hygiene practices
– University Chapter Vice-President

Loaves & Fishes Free Medical Clinic Volunteer [4hours/week]	Feb 2018 - 2019

– Weekly Feeding Ministry that provides free hot meals, worship service, and medical clinic to those in need
– Volunteered for the medical clinic providing blood pressure measurements and preventative care education

Peoria Rescue Ministries Computer education Tutor [4hours/week]	Feb 2018 - 2019

– High Impact volunteer in the Women Recovery programs. A High Impact volunteer is someone who desires to have consistent, personal relationship with clients of Peoria Rescue Ministries.
– Assisted women with basic computer skills and programs such as Microsoft Word, Excel, and PowerPoint

Presence Saint Francis Hospital [3hours/week]	2016

– Direct Patient interaction by delivering drinks and communicating compassion
– Wrote thank you cards for outgoing patient, sanitized/restocked supplies, and interacted with patient families in the waiting room

Unity Point Methodist Hospital Pre-Operation Room & Emergency Department (80 hrs 2015-2016)	2011-2017

– Directed patients to their rooms and constructed a comfortable atmosphere by being attentive to their needs
– Created and redistributed patient's informational charts
– Assisted nurses' daily activities such as folding patients' gowns, sanitizing patients' rooms, restocking, and discharging patients

Evanston Scholars Biology/Anatomy Tutor	2016 - 2017

– Tutor underrepresented high school students in Evanston Township High school on biology and anatomy.

– Offered studying tips and time management

EXTRA-CURRICULAR ACTIVITIES & LEADERSHIP

Illuminate Mentorship Program– President [3 hour/week]	2014-2017

– Illuminate is a mentor/mentee program where undergraduate students are paired with underprivileged high school juniors and seniors to help them with ACT/SAT and college applications
– Initiated, directed, and matched mentors with high school mentees
– Planned and scripted academic study guides and timeline for mentors

MedLife - Vice President [1 hour/week]	2014-2017

– Medical Society provides medical support to third world countries in global brigades
– Executed building relationships with the MedLife committee in Peru to plan brigade trips
– I was a trip leader to the Brigade trip to Cusco, Peru. Assisted physicians, dentists, and pharmacists in mobile clinics.

K-12 School Funding Initiative Bill Reform – Team Leader	2013

– Invited by the director of Legislative Relations and Strategic Planning of IMSA to lead a team of high school students who demonstrate leadership in proposing a solution of the K-12 school funding initiative to Illinois State Senators

Northwestern Club Tennis/KANU Team Soccer - Women's Soccer Team Captain [3 hour/week]	2014-2017

AWARDS
• **Northwestern Weinberg Dean's List**
Fall 2017-2018, Spring 2016-2017, Winter 2016-2017, Fall 2016-2017, Winter 2015-2016, Fall 2015-2016
• **Weinberg Summer Research Grant 2017**
Awarded grant money of $3500 to support current Sleep

Homeostasis independent research for the summer

· Academic Year Undergraduate Research Grant 2017

Awarded grant money of $1000 to support current Circadian Rhythm independent research

· Korean-American Scientists and Engineers Association (KSEA) Scholarship 2017

This award recognizes students in the US who have demonstrated outstanding academic performance, leadership, and community service.

· Korean Honor Scholarship 2017

Awarded to two outstanding students of Korean heritage with high academic achievement and leadership qualities for future professional careers in Midwest states.

· Summer Internship Grant Program (SIGP) 2016

Awarded grant money to support current unpaid summer research

· AP Scholar Award 2014

Awarded for academic outstanding achievement

· The President's Volunteer Service Awards- Gold Award 2012, 2013

Awarded for achieving more than 250 hours of service over a 12-month time period

CHAPTER 4: ORGANIZING THE PREMED TIMELINE

Although the timeline below is not the timeline that I followed precisely, I list a week-by-week schedule below. If you find difficulty creating a schedule, perhaps this tentative timeline will help you to accomplish everything you need to do as a premed applicant. Usually, it takes 2 years to take the MCAT and apply to medical school. Therefore, "#1" represents the first year, and "#2" represents the second year. Theoretically, #1 would be similar to junior year, and #2 would represent someone's senior year.

#1 January: Budgeting and MCAT Brainstorm

1st Week	Start budgeting your medical school journey. Refer to the finances tab. Apply for AAMC Fee Assistance Program (FAP) if you qualify
2nd Week	Schedule an appointment with your premed health adviser and discuss whether you are ready for the MCAT and/or medical school application process. Assess the strength of your application such as GPA, MCAT, research experience, clinical experience, etc.
3rd Week	Buy MCAT prep materials and start MCAT Prep
4th Week	Register for MCAT testing date. Refer to AAMC MCAT testing dates and registration times. A

	popular testing date is in April. MCAT Prep

#1 February: Recommendation Letters & MCAT Prep

1st Week	Brainstorm who you will ask for the letter of recommendation (LOR). MCAT prep
2nd Week	Confirm LOR, MCAT prep
3rd Week-4th Week	MCAT Prep

#1 March: MCAT Prep

1st Week – 4th Week	MCAT Prep

#1 April: MCAT Testing & Rest!

1st Week	Final MCAT Prep
2nd Week	MCAT Test Date!!!
3rd Week	Rest (you deserve it)
4th Week	Rest (you still need it)

#1 May AMCAS Applications & Personal Statement

1st Week	Submit transcript, Begin Primary Statement Brainstorm, Access MSAR subscription
2nd Week	Begin AMCAS Applications, Begin Primary Statement Draft & Work/Activities
3rd Week – 4th Week	Personal Statement

#1 June: Submit Personal Statement & Begin Secondary Essay

1st Week	Finalize Personal Statement & Submit Primary Application. It is important to submit your primary application as soon as it opens!
2nd Week – 4th Week	Prewrite Secondary Applications. Make sure to submit LOR to schools. Some undergradu-

ates will use a recommendation packet or committee letter.

#1 July: Secondary Applications

1st Week-4th Week	Prewrite Secondary Essays and submit. Remember, no applicant will receive MD secondary applications until after July 1st. Remember, your application will only be "ready to be reviewed" until all of the following components have been received: Verified primary application, completed secondary application, LOR, transcript, MCAT score, & Casper test (only certain schools will require Casper).

#1 August: Interview Prep

1st Week	Create outlines to high yield interview questions
2nd Week	Schedule mock interviews
3rd Week	Prepare interview materials (clothes, shoes, portfolio)

#1 September - #2 March

Rock your interviews!

April 30: If holding multiple acceptances, an applicant must choose 1 school. They may hold unlimited number of waitlist schools. If you are on a waitlist, most schools will start moving through the list in late May.

CHAPTER 5: DO VS MD APPLICATION

Many premeds at first do not understand the differences between allopathic and osteopathic schools. Although I spent numerous hours researching the key differences between the two programs during my application season, I did not fully understand it until I attended my interviews. Since medical school interviewers expect applicants to know the differences, I encourage you to know the similarities and differences before writing your personal statement. Therefore, I outlined the similarities and differences of MD vs DO.

After speaking to many physicians and residents, I noticed that many were "politically correct" when they explained the differences between allopathic (MD) and osteopathic (DO) degrees. I was told that:

- "It does not matter if you have a MD or DO degree because you are still a doctor"
- "Patient's only care if you're a doctor. They don't ask if you're a MD or DO doctor"
- "they do the same thing and have similar opportunities regardless what degree you have"

However, if you are like me, you might be more interested in the factual differences between a DM or DO degree. Before I started to research the differences between the two programs, I had the following questions:

1. **What are the similarities of MD and DO programs?**
2. **What are the similarities of MD and DO doctors?**

3. **What are the differences of MD and DO programs?**
4. **What are the differences of MD and DO doctors?**
5. **What scores do I need to be a competitive applicant for MD vs DO programs?**
6. **How will MD vs DO degrees influence residency options?**
7. **How will MD vs DO degrees influence specialty options?**
8. **Are there salary differences between the two programs?**

Before answering these questions, I will give you a brief summary on the two types of medical educations available.

Allopathic (MD)

There are roughly 130-140 allopathic medical schools showcasing the traditional allopathic curriculum which focuses on the diagnosis and treatment of disease. Upon graduation which normally takes 4 years, these students receive the M.D. (Medical Degree) degree[4]. Allopathic medical schools are accredited by the LCME (Liaison Committee on Medical Education). This is the degree that most people are familiar with.

Osteopathic (DO)

There are roughly 30-35 osteopathic medical schools showcasing the osteopathic curriculum which features a complementary approach to the allopathic curriculum. The osteopathic curriculum features specialized training in Osteopathic Manipulative Medicine (OMM) which takes on a more holistic philosophy. The OMM is closely aligned to chiropractic manipulations by making noninvasive skeletal adjustments (cracking of the bone) to realign with the natural body. This is thought to restore health and relieve pain by maintaining the relationship between the body's structure and function. Generally, I have heard students who merely apply to osteopathic schools state that they are looking to go into primary care. They state that they are attracted to learning the OMM methods as it allows physicians to "have some more to offer" to the patients who experience chronic pain. For example, rather than providing pain medications to patients or applying invasive surgeries, I have heard that using noninvasive manipulation can "bring the body back into homeostasis" to treat illnesses and injuries. This is why you will hear that the osteopathy has a "whole body philosophy" that maintains the "natural function of a holistic body." However, when it comes to practice, I'm not sure how much they actually apply these techniques (especially if DO students go into dermatology, general surgery, etc). Osteopathic medical schools are accredited by the Commission on Osteopathic College Accreditation (COCA). Upon graduation, which normally takes 4 years, these students receive the D.O. (Doctor of Osteopathy) degree[4].

What are the similarities of MD and DO programs?

The education and requirements to apply to MD and DO programs are quite similar. For example, students must complete premed prerequisites, MCAT, and have a Bachelor's degree prior to matriculating medical school. In order to be a competitive applicant, students should gain experiences in community service, clinical volunteering, research, and extracurricular activities. Both programs are typically 4 years long.

What are the similarities of MD and DO doctors?

Both are leaders in diagnosing patients, treating patients, and prescribing medications. Both doctors can be licensed to practice medicine in the United States. Both MD and DO graduates can apply to any specialty (however, the acceptance rate is different – more on this later)

What are the differences of MD and DO programs?

DO programs are more likely to accept students from non-traditional backgrounds. A non-traditional applicant includes those who are older, career-changers, or students that have taken significant time off after undergraduate graduation due to unsuccessful medical school applications. If applying to DO schools, then shadowing a DO physician is imperative. If you can obtain a letter of recommendation from a DO physician, then this will help show Osteopathic admissions that you are interested in becoming a DO doctor.

Unlike the MD program, students in the DO program must complete 200 hours of Osteopathic Manipulative Treatment (OMT) as a part of the Osteopathic Manipulative Medicine requirement. Before the residency merger happens in 2020 (more about this later), MD students must pass the USMLE (United States Medical Licensing Exam) to graduate medical school, and DO students must pass the COMLEX (Comprehensive Medical Licensing Examination) to graduate medical school. As indicated earlier, there are approximately 130-140 allopathic medical schools and 30-35 osteopathic medical schools[4].

What are the differences of MD and DO doctors?

While both MD and DO physicians can specialize in any field, MD doctors will be more likely to specialize in fields such as neurology, cardiology, urology, and surgery. MD doctors will tend to work in urban areas. On the other hand, DO physicians will be more likely to practice in primary medicine and work in rural areas. Since DO programs teach OMM, DO doctors will be able to use this approach effectively in primary care. There are approximately 9:1 ratio of MD:DO doctors in U.S[4].

What scores do I need to be a competitive applicant for MD vs DO Programs?

According to AAMC, the average applicant applying to MD programs in 2018-2019 had a MCAT of 505.6, science GPA of 3.47, and a cumulative of 3.57. The average applicant accepted to MD programs in 2018-2019 had a MCAT of 511.2, science GPA of 3.65, and a cumulative GPA of 3.72[5]. In the 2018-2019 cycle, there were a total of 95,797 MD applicants and only 40,174 of the students were accepted. The acceptance rate for allopathic medical schools is 41.9%[6].

The average GPA and MCAT for accepted DO students are significantly lower. According to AACOM, the average applicant accepted to DO programs in 2017 had a MCAT of 503.1, science GPA of 3.43, and a cumulative GPA of 3.53[7]. In the 2017-2018 cycle, there were a total of 20,981 applicants for 7,467 seats[8]. The acceptance rate for osteopathic medical school is 35.6%.

Statistically speaking, it is harder to get into a DO program due to the lower acceptance rate (35.6% DO vs 41.9% MD). However, this data makes sense because there are only 30-35 DO programs compared to the 130-140 MD programs in the United States. Practically speaking, these data indicate that students must score higher on the MCAT and maintain a higher GPA to be a competitive applicant for MD programs.

According to Shemmassian Academic Consulting, they advise students to apply to a mixed number of MD and DO programs depending on their GPA and MCAT scores. They state that if a student has a cumulative GPA of 3.6 with well-written application essays and letter of recommendations, then they should apply to the following distributions of MD and DO schools based on their MCAT scores:

MCAT 510+	100% M.D. Programs	0% D.O. Programs
MCAT 505 – 509	75% M.D. Programs	25% D.O. Programs
MCAT 500 – 504	25% – 50% M.D. Programs	50% - 75% D.O. Programs
MCAT Below 500	0% - 25% M.D. Programs	75% - 100% D.O Programs

(What MCAT Score Do You Need to Get Into Medical School? Shemmassian Academic Consulting (n.d.)) www.shemmassianconsulting.com/blog/mcat/#part-4-where-to-apply-to-medical-school=

If student has higher GPA, then apply a higher percentage of MD programs. If student has lower GPA, then apply to a higher percentage of DO programs[9].

How will MD vs DO degrees influence residency options?

I must emphasize that all DO physicians are fully trained and accredited in all aspects of the allopathic degree. All medical specialties and residencies including surgery residencies may accept both M.D. and D.O physicians; however, it seems that more competitive residencies favor students with a M.D. degree which leaves osteopaths to be at a disadvantage. According to Shemmassian consulting, MD students have a 95% match rate to allopathic residencies while D.O. students have a 70% match rate to allopathic residencies[4].

Currently D.O. and M.D. residencies are matched in different processes. As of March 2019, MD students are matched to residency programs accredited by the Accreditation Council for Graduate Medical Education (ACGME). DO students will be matched to residencies accredited by either ACGME or AOA. In order to match into ACGME, MD and DO students must take the USMLE test. Only DO students take the COMLEX test to apply to AOA residencies. Therefore, the safest way for current DO students to apply to MD residencies is to take both the COMLEX and USMLE.

However, I have heard rumors that the allopathic and osteopathic medical professions are attempting to transition into a single accreditation system of the residency matching system in the near future. I believe that with the merger, all medical students in both MD and DO programs will take one unifying test to match into residency programs. Since the merger has not happened yet, no one knows exactly how this will change the matching process. I also do not know whether this merger will be advantageous or disadvantageous to MD students. However, we can hope that the purpose of the merger is to create a consistent method of evaluating residencies for both DO and MD students.

How will MD vs DO degrees influence specialty options

If you are set on pursuing a specialty, then you will have a higher chance of practicing that specialty as a MD student. Since ACGME accredited residencies tend to train more medical specialists, it makes sense that DO students currently have a harder time pursuing a specialty training. However, with the new merger coming up in 2020, no one knows for sure how this will affect the competitiveness of residency placements.

♠ Of course, DO students who graduate at the top of their class will have a higher chance of being accepted to top osteopathic and allopathic residencies. As you begin to shadow physicians, residents, and medical students, I advise you to ask as many questions as you can. However, also beware that their story is only one data point. For example, I shadowed an anesthesiologist when I was in high school. When I asked him if there were any differences between a MD and DO education, he told me that the difference was negligible because you could become whatever doctor you wanted to become. He pointed at himself as he explained to me that he was an osteopathic physician who specialized in anesthesiology. After listening to his story, I was convinced that there were no differences between the two educations. However, years later, I came to know that that particular DO anesthesiologist scored extremely well on the USMLE and also graduated at the top of his class.

Are there salary differences between the two programs?

My answer to this question is yes and no. On average, allopathic physicians earn higher incomes than DO physicians. However, this is because allopathic physicians tend to specialize and are more likely to live in urban areas which naturally have a higher cost of living. Since more osteopathic physicians tend to practice family medicine or other primary care fields, they are more likely to reside in rural areas. I would assume that osteopathic and allopathic physicians would have similar salaries under equal circumstances[4].

I must also state that there is a fairly pervasive perception that the allopathic curriculum and degree is superior than an osteopathic degree. This is likely due to the fact that most allopathic medical schools have higher average MCAT and GPA scores than osteopathic schools. This stigmatism is also seen in international practice. While all MD physicians have full practice rights internationally (after passing country-specific exams), DO physicians have limited opportunities to practice globally.

Whether these "superiority" arguments are justifiable or not, since the vast majority of physicians have an MD degree, I believe that this has traditionally been the more competitive route to medical school. Needless to say, I believe that the number of Osteopathic physicians are rising which means that the stereotype between allopathic and osteopathic schools will diminish in the near future. Similarly to how the MD and DO residencies are now merging, I am beginning to think that there will be a single medical school system in the future as well.

In summary, I believe that both allopathic and osteopathic medical schools will provide an equally extensive education to train doctors at the highest caliber. Nevertheless, I encourage pre-med students to reflect on their statistics (GPA & MCAT) and consider their future aspirations before deciding if they should apply to MD or DO schools.

CHAPTER 6: MCAT® AND CASPER® PREPARATION

Where to start and how to organize

Everyone knows that they have to take the MCAT at some point in time before applying to medical school. They also believe that they have plenty of time before they need to start thinking about the MCAT; yet, majority of students will be surprised with how fast time flies by. Taking the 7 hour MCAT test is daunting, but I believe that the hardest part about the MCAT is understanding how to study and planning your plan of attack. I believe my lack of organization, preparation, and misunderstanding about the MCAT drove me to take a Gap Year. Although my story of MCAT preparation is just one example, I hope you can take away my strengths and learn from my mistakes and weaknesses so you can prepare for the MCAT more efficiently.

In this section, I will explain when I began studying for the MCAT and how I organized my schedule through a timeline format. I hope this format will show you how early I began to plan for the MCAT and what was going through my head at certain periods of time. For clarity purposes, I will indicate the month and year along with my year in college.

May 2016 | Sophomore

My sophomore year was coming to an end and I knew that I

needed to start thinking about the MCAT. Since I would finish all my premed prerequisite courses at the end of my sophomore year, I did not have to worry about self-learning any unlearned material for the MCAT.

I began thinking when would be the best time to take the MCAT. Since I did not originally plan to take a Gap Year, I thought it would be advantageous to take the MCAT as soon as possible to get it out of the way. Therefore, it was time to choose a testing date that I could perform most optimally. Knowing that I was not a great test taker, I thought it would be smart to take the MCAT as soon as possible in case I would have to retake the exam. I also knew that I wanted to take the test early because I knew it would be difficult balancing college courses with MCAT studying. With these factors in mind, I decided that the most optimal test date was September 2016 (This was the last possible date before the start of my Junior year.) My plan was to spend the summer researching at Northwestern and also prepping for the MCAT.

♠ If you plan to take Organic Chemistry or Physics during Junior year, I would hold off taking the MCAT until the winter or spring of Junior year so you can at least build a solid foundation in those subjects before taking the MCAT. Since I had taken Organic Chemistry during the summer after my freshman year, and also doubled up on Biology and Physics during my sophomore year, this allowed me to complete all my premed prerequisites by the end of sophomore year.

June 2016 | Sophomore

After finishing my sophomore college finals on the 2nd week of June, I was busy with starting my summer research project at the clinical health psychology department at Northwestern. I also went Lima, Peru as a part of a medical missions trip from June 24th - July 2nd. I didn't realize how fast time flew by because June was already over, and I had not started studying for the MCAT.

July 2016 | Summer before Junior Year

After I returned from Peru, I became anxious knowing that I had 2 months left before the September MCAT date. I began to panic because I did not know how to start studying for my MCAT. Therefore, I went to the nearest Barnes & Nobles and decided to buy the Kaplan MCAT book set. Even though I bought the MCAT book, I felt overwhelmed because there were so many contents to cover in a short period of time. I was unsure what I needed to study, and how I needed to study in order to be ready for the September exam.

During the first week of July, I decided to have coffee with one of my close friends who told me that she was taking an online MCAT prep program through PrincetonReview (PR). I'm really glad I had this conversation because I realized that I needed guidance and a structured study plan to study as efficiently as possible. That night, I decided to enroll in a PrincetonReview online MCAT course. I appreciated this program because it had a comprehensive set schedule that would allow me to finish concept review and test preparation before my September MCAT test.

♠ I explain at the end of this chapter why I decided to buy the PrincetonReview Prep Program, and not the Kaplan Prep Program.

My Princeton Review textbooks arrived around July 9th and I began the first online class on July 11th. I was instantly impressed by the structure of the online course. It outlined pre-lecture homework assignments, post-lecture homework assignments, and additional passage-based questions that I could do. All the homework assignments were either multiple choice questions or passage-based questions so I was happy that I was solving MCAT structured questions right off the bat. I knew that if I kept up with the online course which included roughly 35 lectures, then I would be finished with concept review approximately 3 weeks before the September test date. I could then spend the next 3 weeks drilling practice questions.

I still had not registered for the September MCAT test because I wanted to see how I performed on an unofficial practice test before committing. I was also afraid of wasting $315 in the event that I chose not to take the test.

♠ Although I recommend students to register for their upcoming MCAT exam as soon as possible, it is possible to register for the exam 8 days prior to the testing date. Keep in mind that the registration prices increase the later you register[10].

♠ The online program laid out a strict schedule that guaranteed that I would finish concept review in less than 2 months. This pre-structured resource was essential because it helped me save time from having to organize and develop my own schedule. ♠ Make sure that your concept review is finished at least 3-4 weeks before the test date so you have plenty of time solving practice problems and full length tests. Remember to give yourself breaks and catch-up time in your schedule to count for unexpected delays. My school counselor recommends students to set aside 3 months to prepare for the MCAT.

August 2016 | Summer before Junior

I was proud of myself for keeping up with the studying schedule because I had finished all concept review by August 15th. On April 16th, I decided to do my first Princeton Review MCAT practice test. To my immediate dismay, I received a 498. I was utterly shocked and could not believe that all my effort had only given me a 498. I desperately took additional Princeton-Review practice tests, but my scores remained to be around 501-504. I knew that these scores were not competitive enough to get into medical school, especially as an Asian applicant. Ultimately, I decided to postpone the MCAT test date.

*I will explain more on this point later, however, I did not realize until 1 year later, that PrincetonReview tests are often much harder (6-10 points) than the official MCAT test.

♠ It is advised to take the official AAMC practice MCAT test to determine your tentative score. Third party MCAT practice tests (such as PrincetonReview, Kaplan, ExamCrackers, etc) are not representative of the official MCAT score, and often are harder than the official MCAT exam. The purpose of solving third party MCAT tests are to practice your solving ability and to learn from your wrong answers. Therefore, DO NOT gauge your score from these third party practice tests.

September 2016 | Junior

After I decided not to take the exam on September 2016, I wasn't quite sure what to do. I continued to do concept review and solve problems to keep my memory fresh throughout the summer. I began my Junior year at Northwestern and continued to do a couple MCAT passage questions every day to retain my knowledge. To keep my story short here, I overloaded on my college courses to graduate early and ultimately did not take the MCAT during my Junior year.

When June 2017 rolled around after junior year, I decided to restart this MCAT process again. I was a neurobiology student researcher during the summer so I had to balance my commitment as a researcher as well as to prepare for the MCAT. My research commitment lasted until 4pm. Therefore I could start studying after 4pm. Here is my schedule that worked for me:

June 15 – July 15: Review Concept for 6-7 hours daily

Monday, Tuesday, Wednesday	Tuesday, Thursday Schedule	Saturday Schedule	Sunday Schedule

Schedule			
10am-4pm Research 4pm-6pm Break/Dinner 6pm-12:00am MCAT	10am-2:30pm Research 2:30pm-3pm Break 3pm-6pm MCAT 6pm-6:45pm Dinner 7:00-11:30am MCAT	10am-11am Brunch 12-6pm MCAT 6pm-8pm Break/Dinner 8pm-11pm MCAT	Catch up & Rest Day

I think that my concept review was fairly easy because I had finished the PrincetonReview (PR) online course last year. I decided not to enroll in another online course because it was too expensive. Instead, I re-read the prep books and tried to solidify my weak concepts. I still had access to the PR online course and although I couldn't access the lectures anymore, I was able to solve an overwhelming amount of unanswered practice questions. I set myself a strict schedule (refer to the table above) and I'm pretty proud that I stuck to my schedule. Starbucks was my friend because it was open until midnight during the weekdays. I went to Starbucks so frequently that the barista knew my name and my "usual" drink! (I felt honored, but it was honestly pretty sad).

July 15-August 10: Review Concept and Solve questions (6-7 hours daily)

I decided to register for the September 9th 2017 MCAT test date because I wanted to be committed. I also wanted to register early because I wanted to secure my first choice location. I live in a suburb, so this wasn't a huge problem for me; however, I know some friends in urban areas that had to drive 1+ hours because their 1st choice spot was quickly filled. So make sure to reserve your spot as soon as possible if you live in a busy area.

I spent this time solidifying concepts and memorizing equations. I decided to take my first practice test from PrincetonReview and was AGAIN devastated that I got a 503. At this time, I began questioning my own ability and panicked about my future. A couple of days passed (and I feel stupid for realizing this too late), but I decided to ask my premed upperclassmen friends how they compared the Princeton Review MCAT exams to the official MCAT exam. To my immediate surprise, all of my friends commented on how the Princeton Review exams were often 5-10 points more difficult than the official MCAT. If they were correct, this would give me a projected score of 508-513. While this new information gave me a huge relief, I was disappointed at myself because perhaps this simple fact could have saved me from taking a Gap Year. However, I shrugged this regret off and remained optimistic. I knew that the Gap Year allowed me to gain more clinical experiences as a medical scribe and spend more time on my application materials.

♠ The biggest lesson I learned is that third party practice cannot be directly compared to the official AAMC MCAT test. Different companies have varying levels of difficulty and a quick online search can show how other students compared the unofficial tests to the official one. AAMC also offers a couple of free MCAT practice tests that are more comparable to the official MCAT test. Therefore, students should use the AAMC MCAT practice test score to gauge their MCAT score.

August 10-September 4: Practice problems: 7-9 hours daily

I spent the next few weeks doing practice tests. I took approximately 2-3 full length tests a week and spent the next couple of days reviewing missed questions and solidifying weak concepts. For all tests, I imitated similar testing conditions by having ear plugs, paper, and a pencil. I decided to take 2 official AAMC MCAT practice tests about two weeks before my test date and received a 507 and 509 respectively. Although I wasn't too happy with my score, I realized that I rushed on every section. Since I had 10-15 minutes remaining on all sections, I thought that if I slowed down and used the entire allotted time on the actual test, I could reach my goal of about 511-513.

On all practice tests, I thoroughly analyzed my mistakes and made sure that I completely understood what the correct answer was. For the rest of the week, I continued to solve questions and established an equation sheet of all the things I had to memorize. As my test date neared, I tried waking up around 6-7am to develop a morning routine.

September 5-September 8: Rest with minimum review of 2-3 hours daily

My test date was September 9. I decided to limit myself to 2-3 hours of studying for the last couple of days. During this time, I reviewed any material I consistently missed and also memorized my equation sheet. (For the record, you do not receive an equation sheet. Therefore, you need to memorize all chemistry, biology, and physics equations). I was pretty exhausted and burned out by this point so I decided to spend my days hanging out with friends. I slept around 10pm and woke up at 6-7am every day to develop a consistent sleep-wake cycle. On September 8th, I decided to take a quick drive to the testing facility to make sure I knew how to get there. Although I did not feel 100% confident, I could not be more excited to get this thing over with.

September 9: MCAT Day!

I woke up at 5:45am, took a quick cold shower, ate a full breakfast, and drank minimal coffee. I didn't want to drink too much liquid for the fear of constantly needing to go the bathroom during the middle of the test. I arrived to the testing facility by 7:30am. I didn't mind where I sat during my test; although, I wanted to be as far away from the door so I would not be distracted by the constant opening and closing of the doors.

♠ Students are allowed to go in and out of the testing room as long as they are finished with their section. While it would seem that all students use the entire allocated time, many students did not take advantage of the full time. Therefore, students continuously went in and out of the testing room at different periods of time. I felt sorry for the student who had to sit right next to the door because I'm sure the sound of opening and closing of the door would have been a huge distraction. Therefore, I would advise you to arrive around 7:20-7:30am to your testing facility to secure your best seat. I swear, I'm not really an anxious person, but any small noises or distractions will be exaggerated since everyone will be somewhat stressed and anxious during testing day.

The MCAT test finally started and everything went along as expected. The ear plugs I brought were extremely helpful to zone out distracting noise such as coughing, sneezing, or pencil tapping. There was a headset supplied by the test taking facility that students could use; however, it was big and bulky, and it looked incredibly uncomfortable to wear.

After I was finished with each section, I used all the allocated break time to go to the bathroom, stretch, and clear my mind. For lunch, I brought a sandwich, banana, and a granola bar. It was funny that no one talked during the lunch break - I'm sure we were all nervous and exhausted from the test. Although the test was long, it went by quicker than I expected. My first impression was that the test was extremely hard and I thought I would receive about a 506. Any who, I could not be more excited that I had finished!

One month later, I received an email that my MCAT score had been scored and released. My heart immediately jumped and I could feel every individual hair on my body rising up. However, I decided to relax and spent some time creating a score list (such as the one below) prior to checking my score. This table would help me objectively decide whether I was going to keep my score, or retake this test.

IF	THEN
MCAT score is 511 or lower	Absolutely retake the test
MCAT score is 512	I am unsure what I should do, please help because I hate being indecisive

| MCAT score is 513 or higher | Keep your score and do not retake! |

I was anxious as I entered my username and password to reveal my MCAT score. Since I wasn't quite sure what to do if I received a score of 512, I repeated "please not 512, please not 512." And as if the world played a trick on me, my score was exactly 512. Of course, I was happy that I scored higher than my two AAMC MCAT practice tests; however, I started to worry and contemplate whether I needed to retake the exam. The exact breakdown of my score was Biology/Biochemistry: 128, Chemistry/Physics: 129, Cars: 125, Psychology/Sociology: 130. For the next 3 months, I discussed my score with my parents and the Northwestern Pre-med advisor to decide whether I needed to retake the test. After much deliberation, I made the decision to keep my score of 512, and not retake the exam. Below, I list the reasons why I decided not to retake the MCAT.

Overall, I am happy that I decided to wait 1 year before taking the exam. I do not think I was prepared to take the exam right after my sophomore year (September 2016). Waiting to take the MCAT after my junior year (September 2017) allowed me to solve more practice problems and have a deeper understanding of all the concepts. My biggest advice to students is to not rush. This is an important exam that will determine whether or not you will be accepted to medical schools. Therefore, set aside a significant amount of time to study for your MCAT. Although you will never feel completely ready to take the test, it is important to feel confident before taking your exam.

WHY I DECIDED NOT TO RETAKE THE MCAT EXAM

1. **I performed better on the official MCAT test than my practice tests**

   My official score of 512 was significantly higher than both of the AAMC MCAT practice tests which were 507 and 509. The official AAMC practice tests are extremely representative of the official MCAT test. I believe that I was lucky to have performed considerably higher on the official MCAT than my practice tests.

♠ If you performed worse than the AAMC practice tests, then consider to retake the exam. Perhaps anxiety and nervousness masked your true potential, and you believe that you could have performed better.

2. **I feared that I would perform worse on my 2nd MCAT attempt**

   While some medical schools will look at the best MCAT score, most medical schools will look at the most recent MCAT score. Therefore, I was scared at possibly receiving a lower score than my first attempt.

3. **I was realistic that I could not raise my CARS score**

   I was surprised to get a low CARS score of 125; however I knew that reading comprehensive was something I struggled for a long time. In fact, reading comprehensive was also my lowest score on the ACT. This doesn't mean that I gave up on CARS. I probably spent the most time trying to improve my CARS section during my MCAT preparation. Even if I retook the MCAT and managed to raise my CARS section 1-2 points higher, there would be a high chance that 1-2 points may drop in my other sections which would ultimately give me the same overall score of 512. This difference would not make a drastic difference to medical school admissions.

♠ Be realistic of your strength and weaknesses. I knew that CARS would give me the most difficulty so I bought additional books (Examcrackers) to solve as many problems as possible. For those that have always struggled with reading comprehension, I suggest that you take English/literature classes in college to improve reading comprehension and critical analysis. CARS score cannot be increased in a short time period. Therefore, I also suggest that you start to practice solving CARS passages during freshman year in college. Spending 8-10 minutes daily will make a huge difference in the long run. Longterm CARS practice will also increase your reading speed which will become a tremendous advantage to all sections considering that time is extremely limited on the MCAT. Additionally, scoring well on the CARS is important because CARS is an indication of how well you can identify the relationship of important ideas and infer what they imply. Since many believe that reading comprehension and critical analysis is representative of diagnostic ability, perhaps this is why medical admissions weigh heavily on an applicant's CARS score.

4. **Gap in section scores; however, not significant enough**
   My individual MCAT section scores were Biosciences: 128, Chemistry/Physics: 129, CARS: 125, and Psychology/Sociology: 130. As you can see, a section score gap of 3 is present between my lowest two scores (CARS and Biosciences). However, I did not believe that my section gap of 3 would raise a huge red flag in my application. To be a well-rounded test taker, it is optimal to have section scores that are similar to one another.

♠ If you have a large section gap (more than 4-5 points between the two lowest scores) then I would consider retaking the test. Having a large section score difference indicates that you are not well-rounded academically.

5. **My CARS score of 125 is above the required minimum score**
   Some medical schools have required minimum MCAT section scores of either 123 or 124 in order to apply. This means that if you have any sections scores that are under 123 or 124, then they will simply screen out your application without further review. Therefore, make sure to research which medical schools impose a required MCAT score. If your score is lower than this requirement, then retake the test.

6. **My GPA and MCAT scores are balanced**
   My GPA of 3.71 and MCAT score of 512 are balanced and representative of each other. There is often a balanced correlation with GPA and MCAT scores. If your GPA and MCAT are not representative of each other, then this may

be a red flag. For example, a MCAT of 525 and GPA of 3.2 raises questions such as "was the student unmotivated, irresponsible, or lazy." That being said, if you have a GPA of 3.9+ but your MCAT is low, then you should consider improving your MCAT score as high as possible to balance these two scores.

Princeton Review MCAT Prep Program VS Kaplan MCAT Prep Program

MCAT Princeton Review LIVE Online	MCAT Kaplan LIVE Online
Cheaper	3 hours of 1-1 coaching
4 more Prep books with additional CARS practice	Only multiple choice questions on prep books
Passage based practice questions on prep books	
More concept-based questions interspersed to check if concept was understood	
Personal pros: I loved the paper texture of the book because it allowed smooth pencil marks and prevented glares	Personal cons: The paper texture was made from a glossy material which made it hard to write in pencil. This glossy layer also produced glares

In the end, I bought the PrincetonReview MCAT course because I personally liked the structure and format of the book better. I have many friends who chose the Kaplan MCAT course and thought it was better than the PrincetonReview course. There are also many different MCAT prep courses other than Princeton Review or Kaplan; however, I do believe that the two latter options are the most popular. If you compare the prices, Kaplan seemed to be slightly more expensive; however, Kaplan has additional features such as the 1-1 coaching that my friends enjoyed having.

♠ There is an incredible amount of resources to choose from that will meet your needs. Are you a student with a random work schedule and can't attend either in-person or online lectures? Try a self-paced program. Are you someone who is running short on time or need a strict schedule to follow? Try either an in-person or online program. While I understand that spilling roughly $1500-$2000 on a program is not easy, I believe that this MCAT prep prepared me well. I highly encourage you to look into these programs because it is worth it. However, for those on a tight budget, I also understand that investing in a program like this is not always feasible. In this case, I would at least purchase a MCAT book set and start the concept review. There are a ton of free resources online such as Kahn Academy and AAMC. Although it is easy to find small amounts of free practice questions online, it will be difficult to find full length practice tests especially with answers and explanations (which is the most important part.) I encourage you to think of it as an investment and spend some extra bucks buying full length practice tests either online or in a bookstore. This will help save time from having to search credible and nonredundant information online. With the competitiveness increasing every year, you will be at a war with time and resources. Investing a thousand dollars in MCAT prep may save more money in the long run so you don't have to take the MCAT multiple times.

Common MCAT FAQ

I attempted to answer as many questions about the MCAT that have been asked by my underclassmen, friends, and family. For more information about the MCAT, check out the official AAMC website.

Is there an ideal time to take the MCAT?
The biggest rule of thumb is to take the MCAT when you are

ready. Of course, you will never feel completely ready to take this monstrous test; however, most students will feel prepared enough to take the MCAT after 3 months of studying. Since medical school applications begin in June, many premed health advisers will encourage students to take the exam prior to April. This will ensure that the MCAT is be submitted to medical schools in a timely manner. However, my suggestion is that students take the exam during the fall or winter so they have enough time to retake the exam if necessary.

Many examinees take the test more than once. Thus, consider taking the test earlier in the school year to leave you wiggle room to retake the test if needed. I believe that the most ideal time to take the test is at least 6-8 months before applying to medical schools. This will allow you receive your scores, decide if you will re-test, and prepare for taking another shot at the M-CAT. That being said, medical schools will be able to see all of your scores and there are limits to the number of times you can take the test. According to "The MCAT Essentials for Testing Year 2019," an applicant may only hold 1 MCAT appointment at a time. An applicant can only take the MCAT 3 times in a testing year. An applicant can only take the MCAT up to 4 times over 2 consecutive testing years. An applicant can take the MCAT up to 7 times in totality. Immediately after finishing the MCAT, the applicant has the option to grade the MCAT or void the MCAT. Whether an applicant does not complete the MCAT, or decides to void the MCAT, this is still regarded as an attempt[11].

Due to these strict rules, I believe that an applicant should only take the MCAT when they feel that they are ready. This means that the applicant should take the MCAT after completing all premed requirements such as chemistry, biology, biochemistry, organic chemistry, physics, sociology, and psychology. If this is not possible, students should at least take 1 semester of the required course to build a basic foundation before taking the MCAT. Speak to your pre-health advisor to determine if you are prepared to take the MCAT exam.

How Do I Register for the MCAT?

First you will have to create an AAMC account: https://
apps.aamc.org/account/#/login?
hideCreationQs&gotoUrl=https:%2F%2Fconvey.aamc.org%2F
%23%2F&allowInternal=false

Doing a google search of "U.S. MCAT Calendar, Scheduling Dead-
lines, and Score Release Dates" will allow you to see the list
of available test taking dates. All MCAT exams will begin at
08:00am local time. I advise you to register for the MCAT as
soon as possible because the availabilities for testing sites can
fill up quickly[10].

Doing a quick google search of "AAMC MCAT" will bring
you to the website where you can register for the
MCAT: https://students-residents.aamc.org/applying-medical-
school/taking-mcat-exam/

Below is a table taken from the AAMC website that shows three
scheduling zones and the exam prices: Gold, Silver, and Bronze.
The table also lists the rescheduling fee and cancellation refund.

Scheduling Fees (in USD)

All deadlines are at 7:59 a.m. local test center time on the day of the deadline.					
Gold Zone Deadline: 29 days prior to exam date*		Silver Zone Deadline: 15 days prior to exam date*		Bronze Zone Deadline 8 days prior to exam date*	
Initial Registration	$315	Initial Registration	$315	Initial Registration	$370
Date and/or Test Center Reschedule Fee**	$95	Date and/or Test Center Reschedule Fee**	$155	*No Reschedule Option*	*N/A*
Cancellation Refund	$155	*No Cancellation Refund*	*N/A*	*No Cancellation Refund*	*N/A*
International Fee (if test	$110	International Fee**	$110	International Fee**	$110

taken at international countries)						

MCAT Scheduling Fees. AAMC, (2019). Retrieved from https://aamc-orange.global.ssl.fastly.net/production/media/filer_public/ea/55/ea5574b3-c544-4958-87e2-5b6cf7ac6186/essentials_2019_-final_02072019.pdf

How is the MCAT scored?

The MCAT consists of 4 scored multiple-choice sections: Biological and Biochemical Foundations of Living Systems Section, Chemical and Physical Foundations of Biological Systems Section, Psychological, Social, and Biological Foundations of Behavior Section, and Critical Analysis and Reasoning Skills Section. Each of the section is scored on a scale score ranging from 118 (lowest) to 132 (highest). Adding up the scores of all 4 sections will create a cumulative score of 472 to 528. This score is based on the number of questions answered correctly. There is no penalty for wrong answers or unanswered questions. The 50th percentile of the MCAT test is a score of 500[12].

Additional MCAT Informational Resources

How to Create a Study Plan for the MCAT Exam (AAMC)
https://www.aamc.org/em/marketing/
documents/2019studyplan.pdf

The MCAT Essentials for Testing Year 2019 (AAMC)
https://aamc-orange.global.ssl.fastly.net/production/media/
filer_public/af/5c/af5c52a7-3e4a-4f61-889e-a5edd7490e5e/
essentials_2019_final_10152018.pdf

What's on the MCAT Exam (AAMC)
https://aamc-orange.global.ssl.fastly.net/production/media/
filer_public/44/e8/44e8b9aa-5000-490c-8a6a-c7ff8d01874d/
combined_mcat-content_new_013118.pdf

Khan Academy Test Prep
https://www.khanacademy.org/test-prep/mcat

CASPer® Prep

The CASPer® test (a trademark of Altus Assessments) is a relatively new test that medical schools have started to implement. The CAS-

Per® test was originally developed in Canada to screen for "people skills" by an online situational judgment test. Unlike an IQ test, CASPer® tests for communication, collaboration, empathy, motivation, and ethnic skills to name a few. Although it is an online written test that can be taken at your home, you are not allowed to use any outside resources. In order to monitor this, you must use a computer with a camera which will film you throughout the entire 90 minutes of the test. To clarify, the CASPer® test is a written test (not a verbal test) where you will be typing your answer in the appropriate boxes.

Many people say that you can't prepare for the CASPer® test because it's a personality test. While certain aspects of this statement may be true, I believe that you can practice and prepare for it. Here is my experience with prepping for CASPer®.

Some medical schools do not process the secondary application until the CASPer® test is taken. Since not all schools require CASPer®, I had to research what schools required/recommended the exam. Every year, more schools are adding this requirement in their application. Below you will find a table that lists medical schools that required/recommended CASPer®[13]:

Albany Medical College	Central Michigan University	Drexel University	Florida Atlantic University
Medical College of Georgia Augusta	Medical College of Wisconsin	Mercer University	New York Medical College
Quillen College of Medicine	Rosalind Franklin University	Rutgers University	Stony Brook University
SUNY Upstate Medical University	Temple Lewis Katz School of Medicine	Texas A&M University	Texas Tech University
Tulane University	University of Colorado Denver Medical School	University of Illinois at Chicago	University of Michigan
University of Mississippi	University of Texas Medical Branch Galveston	University of Texas San Antonio	University of Vermont
University of Washington	Virginia Commonwealth University	West Virginia University	

Schools and Programs. CASPer, (n.d). Retrieved from https://takecasper.com/schools-and-programs/

Although most people tend to take the CASPer® test around July of their application process, I decided to take the test earlier just in case I would want to re-take it. However, you do not receive any feedback including your scores (which I personally think is weird. I mean, if they require you to pay and take a test, shouldn't they release your scores?) Anyway, since you do not get to know how you performed on the test, the only reason students retake the test is if they did not answer all the questions due to a lack of time.

I wasn't quite sure when I was going to take the CASPer® test but I decided to buy "Multiple Mini Interview (MMI): Winning Strategies from Admissions" written by Samir Desai. Since the CAS-Per® exam was similar to an MMI interview (which I talk more about on the interview chapter), I bought this book on April 1st and started going through it. Although this book focused on how to successfully go through the MMI interview process, there were many practice questions and "how to formulate an answer" examples that seemed helpful for the CASPer® exam.

On April 19th, I decided to sign up for the earliest CAS-Per ®exam date which was May 15th. I reserved and paid a registration fee of $60 (+$10 on each medical school that the CASPer® score is sent to) and started looking for free resources online. Although there were some videos and free practice tests online, I could not find many resources that came with answers. While there is no "correct answers" to this personality test, there are answers that are better than others. So I decided to buy the Astroff's Prep for CASPer® Package for $150 which gave me 2 Prep courses with questions and answers, and 4 simulated practice tests (without answers). I went through these practices from May 1st-May 14th which I think was plenty of time to practice. It's difficult to truly prepare for these tests because you don't know what the questions will be. In this sense, I think it is a personality test because many situations ask "what would you do in this situation". Although I'm not sure if paying for the CAS-Per® Prep Packages were worth it, I think it was still beneficial that I could have full length practice tests. It was also beneficial for me because I could estimate how much time I could spend on each question.

Format of CASPer® Test

· 90 minute test with optional 15-minute break halfway through

· 12 sections of video and word-based scenarios

· Each scenario has 3-4 questions that must be answered under 5 minutes[13]

♠ You are only given 5 minutes to answer 3-4 follow-up questions so it is important to use your time wisely. Since the CAS-Per® test is a relatively new test, no one knows exactly how much weight the admissions give to the CASPer® exam. Since CASPer® does not release their scores to the applicant, it is difficult to gauge your performance on the exam. However, I believe that there are a couple red flags that you should make note of:

1) If you leave questions blank because you ran out of time.
2) If you answer the question inappropriately and unprofessionally.

The most important reason to practice and prepare for this test is to know how to allocate and use your time wisely. Otherwise, there is no other reason to stress on this test. It is only 90 minutes and if you just give "appropriate answers" to each question, then you will be fine. The hardest part of this test is making sure all answers are answered evenly. For example, you have 5 minutes to answer 3 separate questions. All answers should be at a similar length and quality so make sure that you don't spend too much time on any given question. My college pre-med counselor also told me that CASPer® tests do not weigh too much in the selection process. She told me that I should not worry as long as there are "no red flags" in my answers. So, don't stress too much on this exam!

CHAPTER 7: WHAT IT MEANS TO BE AN ASIAN APPLICANT

The discussion of race in admissions has become an extremely controversial topic these days especially with the onset of recent lawsuits which discussed whether undergraduate admissions were intentionally discriminating against Asian-American applicants. Whether this lawsuit was right or wrong will not be discussed in this book; rather, I would like to discuss if ethnicity plays a role in medical school admissions.

I must admit that throughout my undergraduate and medical school application process, my friends and I repeatedly discussed if the entire application process was fair. We exchanged questions such as "Is it harder to be accepted to school as an Asian applicant?," "Is it fair that Asians (extremely of the Korean, Japanese, Chinese descent) are not considered a minority in the medical application system?," "Would it help us if we don't indicate our race in our applications?." Overall, I had noticed that many of my Asian friends scored higher on the GPA and MCAT scores than the average medical school applicant, and was surprised when many were not accepted to medical school. Therefore, I decided to analyze the data that was published from AAMC to understand what it means to be an Asian-American applicant in the medical school application process. The data that was published from AAMC have generalized the academic performance of individuals from certain ethnic backgrounds. Of course, it is noteworthy to state that there is great variance in performance within ethnic groups, and that there are both high-achieving and low-achieving applicants in every ethnic group. My objective in writing this section is to help you understand the role of ethnicity in medical school admissions and how this knowledge can be used to your advantage during your application process.

Does race play a role in medical school admissions?

While it is difficult to analyze if there is a clear correlation between race and acceptance rates, there seems to be a distinct pattern between ethnicities and their academic performance. For example, I believe that it is harder to get into medical school as an Asian applicant when looking strictly at MCAT and GPA scores. Let's check out the acceptance rates of each ethnic groups that scored an average GPA of 3.4 - 3.59 and MCAT score of 508-512. The table below is an aggregated data from 2013-2016. Old MCAT scores were converted to new MCAT scores based on percentile ranks for your convenience. As you can observe, Asian applicants had the lowest acceptance rate (40.3%) compared to other ethnic groups[15].

Acceptance Rate of each Ethnic Group with a GPA of 3.4 - 3.59 and MCAT of 508-512 (2013-2016)

Ethnicity	Acceptance Rate
Asian	40.3%
White	48.0%
Black or African American	86.9%
Hispanic or Latino	75.9%

Table A-24: MCAT and GPA Grid for Applicants and Acceptees by Selected Race and Ethnicity, 2013-2014 through 2015-2016 (Aggregated), AAMC, (n.d.). https://www.aamc.org/data/facts/applicantmatriculant/157998/factstablea24.html

There seems to be a larger difference between the acceptance rates of various ethnicities with lower MCAT and GPA scores. For example, consider this acceptance rate of various ethnic groups with a GPA of 3.2 - 3.39 and MCAT score of 502 – 506. While approximately 75% of Black or African American students were accepted with a GPA of 3.2 - 3.39 and a MCAT score of 502 – 506, only 14% of Asian students were accepted with similar scores[14]. Therefore, Black and African-American students have the highest chance of being accepted to medical schools with lower scores. If you are an Asian-American or White applicant with these scores, I would recommend you to retake your MCAT test or attend a Post-Bacc program to become a more competitive applicant.

Acceptance Rate of each Ethnic Group with a GPA of 3.2 - 3.39 and MCAT of 502-506 (2013-2016)

Ethnicity	Acceptance Rate
Asian	14.4 %
White	19 %
Black or African American	75.3%
Hispanic or Latino	42.8 %

Table A-24: MCAT and GPA Grid for Applicants and Acceptees by Selected Race and Ethnicity, 2013-2014 through 2015-2016 (Aggregated), AAMC, (n.d.). https://www.aamc.org/data/facts/applicantmatriculant/157998/factstablea24.html

Are Medical School Hesitant to Accept Asian-American students?

While some can argue that medical schools may be hesitant to accept Asian-American applicants with lower MCAT and GPA scores, I believe that medical schools are generally not reluctant to accept Asians. For example, the acceptance rate of each ethnicity within each group is approximately the same. According to the table below, there is approximately 40% acceptance rate within Asian, White, and Hispanic ethnic groups[15]. To be more clear, this means that Asian applicants have a 40% chance of being selected from a pool of Asian applicants. This same principle applies for White applicants and Hispanic/Latino applicants. Interestingly, this data indicates that Black/

African American applicants actually have the lowest probability of being selected from their pool. Overall, this data suggests that Medical School admission officers are not necessarily hesitant to accept Asian-American students compared to other ethnic groups. Perhaps this means that you must score in the top 40% in your ethnic group to be accepted into medical school. Rather than competing against all students, one can say that it's only a competition against your own ethnic group.

Applicants & Acceptees within Ethnic groups (2018-2019)

Ethnicity	Total Applicants	First-Time Applicants	Acceptees
Asian	5871	4510	2674
White	11776	9121	5573
Black or African American	2872	1900	970
Hispanic or Latino	1701	1253	696

Table A-12: Applicants, First-Time Applicants, Acceptees, and Matriculants to U.S. Medical Schools by Race/Ethnicity, 2015-2016 through 2018-2019, AAMC, (n.d.). https://www.aamc.org/download/321480/data/factstablea12.pdf

Acceptance Rate within Ethnic group (2018-2019)

Ethnicity	Acceptance Rate
Asian	44.1 %
White	45.4 %
Black or African American	36.0 %
Hispanic or Latino	42.5 %

Table A-12: Applicants, First-Time Applicants, Acceptees, and Matriculants to U.S. Medical Schools by Race/Ethnicity, 2015-2016 through 2018-2019, AAMC, (n.d.). https://www.aamc.org/download/321480/data/factstablea12.pdf

So is it really harder for Asians to be accepted into Medical School compared to other ethnicities?

While medical schools are not reluctant to accept Asians applicants, it is inarguable that Asians have higher academic standards than other ethnic groups. While an argument can be made that all ethnic groups have an equal acceptance rate of approximately 40%, this argument does not include the differences in MCAT and GPA scores that must be achieved by students. The table below displays the average MCAT and GPA for accepted students based on their ethnic groups. The data indicates that Asians will have to compete with the group that holds the most competitive scores. The data indicates that an Asian applicant should score higher than a 513 MCAT and 3.76 GPA to increase their odds of getting accepted[16].

Disclaimer: Although a pattern can be observed, there is no correlation that can be achieved because standard deviations were not calculated.

Average MCAT and GPA for accepted students based on Ethnic group (2018-2019)

Ethnicity	MCAT	Overall GPA
Asian	513.4	3.76
White	511.9	3.75
Black or African American	505.1	3.51
Hispanic or Latino	506.0	3.60

Table-18: MCAT Scores and GPAs for Applicants and Matriculants to U.S. Medical Schools by Race/Ethnicity, 2018-2019. AAMC, (n.d.). https://www.aamc.org/download/321498/data/factstablea18.pdf

Is this all fair?

The discussion of its fairness is a loaded question. Overall, I believe that it's extremely difficult to answer this question because there are many confounding variables. For example, perhaps race may be strongly associated with socioeconomic status (SES) or those who are underrepresented in medicine (URM). SES describes a person's social standing based on their income, education, and occupation. Therefore, it is unknown if there is a relationship with admissions based on an applicant's SES or URM status. Perhaps a study that compares SES with acceptance rates would give us a more definite answer.

In addition, it is worth understanding the US population of Asians with the number of Asians accepted to medical school in general. From an educated guess, we can assume that the percentage of Asians in the United States is around 4-7%. According to AAMC, approximately 21.3% of medical school applicants were comprised of Asians[15]. I believe that this value is impressive considering that the percentage of Asians accepted in medical school is far greater than of the percentage of Asians in the United States. I am certainly glad that medical schools do not try to reflect the US population statistics when accepting Asians. Therefore, in this regard, the process may be deemed fair.

The Importance of Diversity in Medical School Admissions.
Overall, I believe that it is necessary that medical schools admit a diverse applicant pool by practicing holistic admissions. Since US has a diverse patient population, I believe that having a diverse physician population will better serve and understand the patients. Merely accepting the top performing students with high MCAT and GPA would not be the solution to effective patient care. Differences in personality traits, experiences, occupation, or abilities are important types of diversity; however, I believe that ethnicity is an even more integral aspect of diversity. Therefore, I believe it's understandable why medical school admissions practice race-conscious admissions and ask students to indicate their ethnicity on the application.

How should I use this information to my advantage?
We came to the conclusion that racial differences does come into play when applying to medical school. However, this does not mean that you will not have a chance in medical school acceptance if you are part of the ORM (over-represented in Medicine). Last time I checked, there were plenty of White and Asian-American students in medical school. Furthermore, do not give up if you do not belong in the top 40% of your ethnic pool. There is a reason why admissions do not only accept the

top academic performing students. If this were to be the case, then diversity would be extremely limited.

Therefore, brainstorm how you can make your application stand out as an Asian applicant or a White applicant. Rather than feeling discouraged because you are a "majority," I encourage you to ask yourself "How can I use my background to my advantage to discuss about my personal narrative in a way that promotes the schools mission statement or diversity?" You will have the opportunity to share your personal background and journey in the personal statement, Work and Activities section, and secondary application. With these three large writing components to discuss your unique stories, your application will no longer be just about your race, GPA, and MCAT scores.

In order to become a compelling candidate and distinguish yourself from other applicants, you must show them who you are, what you have done, and why you will become a better doctor than others. Sharing your experience is the only way to be clear of your intentions and passions. It is extremely difficult to share your story if you don't have anything to share. Therefore, find experiences and indulge in opportunities that you are passionate about. Understand how you can apply your strengths and unique traits in an activity to make it your own.

To give you an example, I became a scribe in the Emergency Department after graduating from Northwestern University. I wasn't quite sure how becoming a scribe could be used to my advantage especially because scribing as a premed student wasn't anything unique. However, the more I reflected on myself and the experiences I gained as a scribe, I noticed how I could make this seemingly ordinary gap year experience into an extraordinary eye-opening experience. I decided to share a story of how my ethnic and cultural background had allowed me to partake in an experience that no one else could have. The excerpt below describes a time during my scribing experience that I discussed in my secondary application.

As a medical scribe, I had an opportunity to translate for an elderly Korean woman who refused to receive a blood transfusion. Attributing the patient's fear to a language barrier, I was driven to facilitate the patient in obtaining adequate healthcare. After a lengthy discussion in Korean, it was apparent that the patient depended on oriental medicine and was unfamiliar with the practices of Western medicine. Luckily, my yearly trips to South Korea and my understanding of oriental medicine philosophies from my grandmother, a retired Korean Pharmacist, enabled me to internalize the patient's concerns and relay her cultural ideologies to the physician. Under careful guidance of the physician, I used my native fluency in Korean with my limited, yet familiar knowledge in oriental medicine to gain her trust and articulate the idea of receiving a blood transfusion along with her daily herbal regimen. This experience prompts me to embrace my unique culture and expertise, apply these elements to patient-advocacy, and bring greater perspective during classroom discussions. Whether I am participating in the Student-Run Free Clinic, caring for patients during clinical rotations, or cultivating a learning community with diverse students, I am thrilled to contribute my ethnic background and cultural awareness to further XXX Medical School's mission of transforming medicine and advocating for the wellbeing of our patients.

Now it is time to think about how you can use your ethnic background to your advantage to discuss about your personal narrative in a way that promotes the schools mission statement or diversity. Your experiences do not have to be grand. You do not have to travel half way across the country to serve and you do not have to join the peace corp. Reflect on your experiences no matter how big or small it is and use it to describe your story.

Stating your race is optional. Is it better not to indicate my race on the application?

I do not know the definite answer to this question because I do not know any correlations between the accepted rates of students who indicated their race on the application and those who did not. Quite frankly, I do not know why indicating your race is optional. Perhaps it's the AAMC's method of trying to be as neutral and controversy-avoiding as possible. Regardless of its intentions, I believe that you should not be afraid to hide your identity. First of all, you should be proud of who you are and I do not want you to hide your identity or change your identity. You cannot change your race so might as well own it. Second of all, if you have a common racial last name, then it will be difficult to hide. For example, if I were to be on the admissions team and I saw a last name that was "Kim" or "Park," I would automatically think that this applicant was Korean without hesitation. Third of all, some secondary applications require you to submit your picture. In summary, I do not see a point in trying to hide yourself because your race will become obvious one way or another. Might as well use it in your advantage and be proud of who you are.

Which Medical Schools accept more Asian Applicants?

According to AAMC's study called "Undergraduate Institutions Supplying 50 or More Applicants to U.S. Medical Schools, 2018-2019," the top 10 medical schools with the most Asian medical students include the following in chronological order [17].

1. University of California-Los Angeles
2. University of California-Berkeley
3. University of California-San Diego
4. University of Texas at Austin
5. University of Michigan-Ann Arbor
6. University of Washington
7. Rutgers University
8. The University of Texas at Dallas
9. University of California-Davis

10. University of California-Irvine

As you can see from the list, medical schools in California seems to have the most Asian medical students. These data also makes sense because there are almost 3 to 10 times the number of Asian applicants in California compared to different states. Unfortunately, if your legal residence is not California, then it will be extremely difficult to be accepted to these California public schools. Therefore, consider applying to the following 10 private medical schools with the most Asian medical students[17].

1. Washington University in St. Louis
2. Emory University
3. Cornell University
4. Johns Hopkins University
5. Duke University
6. New York University
7. Rice University
8. Case Western Reserve University
9. Stanford University
10. Boston University

CHAPTER 8:
GLOBAL MEDICAL
MISSIONS TRIP

On June 2017, I went to a global medical brigade to Lima, Peru for one week through the MedLife Program. It was extremely enjoyable that on January 2019, I went to another international medical trip to Antigua, Guatemala for 1 week through the Nivel Maximo Program. Although this medical brigade was equally as enjoyable, I began to realize if these trips were actually meaningful in the way that I wanted it to be. After much thought, I am still unsure if pre-med students should or should not attend medical brigade trips. What I do believe is that the answer depends on the students' underlying intentions, level of cultural competency, personal values, and general level of awareness. I hope that you can make an informed decision on your own by understanding the pros and cons to medical brigade trips.

PROS

Gain Perspectives & Broaden Healthcare Exposure
Attending the trip allows you to step out of your comfort zone and meet people from different cultural, social, and economic backgrounds. In order to understand a culture, you must immerse yourself in it. This trip will also enhance your understanding of healthcare systems in different countries.

Clinical Experience

Assisting doctors, nurses, dentists, and pharmacists will enhance your clinical experience. Whether you are measuring vitals, assisting a procedure, educating personal hygiene, or documenting charts, I believe that this trip can help confirm your passion for medicine. Since I recommend students to have 200+ hours of clinical experience, volunteering abroad will increase your clinical experience hours.

Service Component

You can't change the world, but you can help one person at a time. Many believe that medical brigade trips are unimportant and unnecessary because it cannot leave a lasting change in the community. However, I do not serve with the purpose of changing the community. Rather, I serve with the mindset of helping and comforting one person at a time. By attending this trip and supporting global medical organizations, you will be able to provide healthcare to patients who would otherwise not have access to it.

Character-Building

Serving others can foster characteristics such as compassion, selflessness, sympathy, and a general concern for others.

Travel/Tour

We can't forget about traveling! Since most of the volunteering occurs during the first half of the day, you will have the rest of the day to tour the area. Some volunteers also tend to stay a couple more days after the program to visit touristy spots of the country.

New and Fun!

I believe that attending a medical trip was refreshing from the usual hospital volunteering I did in the United States. I loved the change of scenery and being able to build relationships with teammates and those who had a passion for traveling.

<u>CONS</u>

Expensive

Unless you are in the AmeriCorps or Peace Corps program (in which you get paid), attending medical brigade trips can get expensive. For example, below is a list of fees you may be responsible for in a 1 week brigade package:

- Participation fee ($500 - $1,000)

  This fee may cover registration, limited meals, transportation, and lodging. It can also fund for staff salaries and medical supplies.

- Flight ($400-900)

  Flight costs are normally not included in the participation fee and will have to be paid out of pocket. Ask the brigade program if there are any group discount programs.

- Travel Insurance ($20-$100)

  The cost of travel insurances will vary depending on the packages. Travel insurances may or may not be required; however, it is generally recommended because anything could happen!

- Personal Costs ($200 - $400)

  The personal costs will vary depending on what you spend. Bring enough with you if you are hoping to hit some touristy spots, eat at local restaurants, or buy souvenirs.

Savior Complex

Do not be misguided and believe that you will make a huge difference by attending a medical brigade trip for merely one week.

Ethnical Issues

Some countries do not have strict restrictions or policies that prevent foreigners from practicing medicine. Therefore, this poses to be an ethical problem if untrained students provide healthcare in another country even if they receive consent from the patients.

Temporary Help

Some argue that natives will never develop their own health-care system because they are dependent on foreign aid. They also believe that providing temporary care will not help na-tives in the long run. Therefore, make sure to volunteer for an organization that provide continuous long-term relationships with natives. Additionally, try to find an organization that part-ners with native doctors who speak the language and under-stand the community's cultures.

Limited Help

Many students believe they will "do a lot" in the missions trip only to find out that they are limited in what they can do due to the cultural and language barrier. Unless you are fluent in the language, the language barrier will prevent you from communi-cating with patients and "helping them."

Help needed in your own community

There are plenty of opportunities to be involved in your local community and help the people around you.

Overall, I believe that global medical missions trips sound im-pressive and think that premed students should attend brigade trips if they have the opportunity to do so. As an undergraduate student, we don't have many opportunities to travel or learn about other cultures. Therefore, attending medical brigade trips allow students to gain broader perspectives while also enhancing their resume. If you decide to attend a medical bri-gade trip, I encourage you to gain additional information so you know exactly what to expect. Understanding the pros and cons listed here can allow you to make an informed decision. Per-sonally, I believe that attending a medical trip was an amazing learning opportunity that allowed me to see a larger part of the world we live in. It taught me the importance of preventative care and the severity of a lack of healthcare access around the world. Assisting in the clinic allowed me to gain a deeper appreciation of different cultures and understand the importance of knowing a patient's circumstance before claiming a diagnosis. I believe that this comprehensive exposure to diversity and the opportunity to practice cultural competency will be essential for any students striving to be an attentive and skillful physician.

CHAPTER 9: FINANCE

Potential Expenses

Let's be real, there are more to it than just good grades, good MCAT score, good experiences, and good essays to get into medical school. The entire application process is expensive. However, there are numerous routes of spending. I am pretty certain that no two applicants have spent the exact same amount. Medical school is expensive, and so is the application process.

The expense of applying to medical school will be extremely different based on the number of medical schools you apply too; however, I will show you a couple of different financial spending routes. For those who qualify for AAMC's Financial Assistance Program (FAP) will benefit greatly from this program.

Extremely Economical Flight (with FAP)

Object	Cost ($)	Notes
MCAT Books + Free MCAT Official Prep Products	100-200	Used; The Free MCAT Prep Products are $236 value that can only be given to those with FAP
MCAT Test[10]	125	FAP discount applied
MSAR subscription[18]	0	Free MSAR subscription for 1 year
AMCAS	0	Waiver for all AMCAS fees up to 20 schools.
Secondary Application	500	FAP will cover for about 15-20 schools. If schools do not take FAP, they will lower the secondary fee
Interview Expenses (transportation, shelter, food)	600	Assumes 5 interviews that are local places. Sleep either with friend or through the student host program. Look for discounted hotel prices
Interview clothes	150	Might need some new shoes, or top. Try to borrow clothes
Total	**~ $1,500**	

Economical Flight (without FAP)

Object	Cost ($)	Notes
MCAT Books	100-300	Used books
MCAT Test[10]	315	
MSAR subscription[18]	28	
AMCAS	1000	Assumes 25 school applications
Secondary Application	2500	Assumes 20-25 secondary fees
Interview Expenses	2000	Sleep with a friend or through the student host program. Cheap flights for interviews that are farther away. Assumes 5-7 interviews
Interview Clothes	200-400	Borrow clothes or buy new clothes
Total	**~ $6,500**	

First Class (without FAP)

Object	Cost ($)	Notes
MCAT Review Course	2000-3000	Kaplan and Princeton Review have great courses. Buy additional books & flashcards for extra practice, Admissions consultant who helps with essay editing and mock interviews
MCAT Test[10]	315	
MSAR Subscription[18]	56	Assumes 2 years worth of subscription. Buying MSAR during early Junior year will aid in researching schools early.
AMCAS	1500	Assumes application to 35 schools $170 for 1st school, $39 for additional
Secondary Application	3000	Assumes to 30-35 secondary fees Average $90
Interview Expenses	5000	3-star hotel, uber rides, food, Flights for interviews farther away. Assumes 10-13 interviews
Interview Clothes	400	New suit, dry cleaning, new shoes
Total	~ **$ 13,000**	Eek!

♠ There are clearly huge differences in the 3 spending summaries. The last table reflects approximately how much money was invested throughout my medical school application journey. I'm actually in shock right now because I did not realize how much money was actually spent. Ouch! Luckily, my parents helped pay for half of the total amount so I was super blessed to have their financial support!

Although I recognize that $13,000 was an incredible amount of money invested in my medical school journey, I believe that I would not have been able to receive multiple medical school acceptances without this investment. Each expense helped pave a path for me and I am extremely thankful that I had my parent's support every day. However, I would like to state that the medical school application process is becoming more difficult and competitive with every passing year. More than 50% of the student applicants are not accepted during their first application process meaning that they will try again. Since I had friends applying to medical schools as their 2nd or even 3rd attempt, I wanted to go big or go home. Therefore, you might as well spend a lot of money to be accepted in the 1st try, because applying for the 2nd or 3rd time will end up being more expensive. Of course, this food for thought will only be applicable if one has the financial means to do so. I do want to state that there are more economical paths to the medical application journey. The 2nd table shows a more financially reasonable way to be a successful applicant!

Financial Aid Information Resources
- AAMC Fee Assistance Program: https://www.aamc.org/students/applying/fap/
- AAMC Financial Options: https://students-residents.aamc.org/applying-medical-school/preparing-med-school/paying-medical-school/
- AACOMAS Application Fee Waivers: http://www.aacom.org/become-a-doctor/financial-aid

Financial Aid & Scholarships

To be considered for federal student aid, you must complete a free application for FAFSA that is available after October 1 (after medical school applications are submitted). It is advised to fill out FAFSA as soon as it is released in the beginning of October. However, it is especially advised to complete the FAFSA before February because the medical school financial aid deadline will be around March – April. The requirements for financial aid application will vary for all medical schools; however, each school will usually require you to submit the FAFSA and a school specific financial aid application. If you submit these materials by March, then you will be sent a financial award package by mid-April. If you are a student who will be choosing a school based on financial aid, then it will be crucial for you to submit the financial aid material in a timely manner.

With FAFSA, there are two different types of aid: federal aid and institutional aid. If you would like to qualify for institutional aid which may include both financial-need and merit based aid, then you will have to include your parent's financial information on your FAFSA. Although you are considered an adult and independent from your parents, if you want to apply for any scholarships from the school, you must include your parent's information on the FAFSA. This is a requirement for all medical schools.

Since the financial aid deadline is March or April, you should complete the requirements for all the schools you are considering to attend. This will include both accepted and wait-list schools. It is noted that if you are accepted, then you will be sent a financial aid application reminder via email. Unfortunately, not all waitlisted schools will send the financial aid requirement email which means that you will have to be more proactive in searching their requirements and deadline. If you have any questions, email the financial aid office and they will assist you in making sure all the materials have been submitted.

After your financial aid materials have been submitted to your medical school, you might consider applying to some external scholarships. While some scholarships require that you are "currently enrolled" as a student, you will have to look for scholarships that allow you to apply as long as you have been accepted to a school. Try to search for scholarships online and on medical school's financial websitess which includes some noteworthy scholarships. There are many different scholarships with particular requirements such as "must be living in a rural area" or "must have a Korean decent." Therefore, search for all sorts of different scholarships that you might fall in! Here is a list of scholarships that I have found from my personal search:

Scholarship Prior to Attending

Daughters for American Revolution
A $5,000 scholarship awarded to one student who has been accepted into or who are pursuing an approved course of study to become a medical doctor (no pre–med, veterinarian, or physician assistant) at approved, accredited medical schools, colleges, and universities. The scholarship is not automatically renewable; however, applicant may

reapply for up to four years. Due February 15th. There are 3 scholarships in the following link: https://www.dar.org/national-society/scholarships/nursing-medical-scholarships

The Korean American Scholarship Foundation

This organization awards scholarships of $1,000 to $5,000 to full-time students of Korean heritage enrolled in a 4-year college, university, or graduate and professional school in the Midwest region. If extra funds are available, other students (non-Korean) may qualify for some scholarships. Inquiries and applications are accepted after April 1st with an early July deadline date. For more information and application visit http://kasf.org/application.

Illinois Hospital Research & Educational Foundation

The Illinois Hospital Association, through the Illinois Hospital Research & Education Foundation, awards a number of scholarships throughout the state each year to students pursuing their education in health-related fields of study. Completed application and references must reach IHREF by APRIL 15, 2015. https://www.team-iha.org/member-resources/constituency-sections/constituency-on-volunteers-resources

Scholarship during MS1

White Coat Investor:

https://www.whitecoatinvestor.com/scholarship

Chinese American Scholarship

Do not have to have a Chinese heritage: https://camsociety.org/scholarship/

Chinese American Physicians Society:

http://www.caps-ca.org/
http://www.caps-ca.org/scholarship.html

Wellesley College Scholarships

Two scholarships are available for women medical students. Applications and instructions may be found at website. M.A. Cartland Shackford Medical Fellowship-Applicants may be graduates of any US college and be enrolled in any accredited US medical school. The award amount is $11,000 "for the study of medicine with a view to general practice, not psychiatry." Sarah Perry Wood Medical Fellowship-Available to Wellesley graduates only who are accepted or enrolled in a medical program. Award amount up to $71,000. Application deadline: December 1.

Tylenol Future Care Scholarship
Apply after 1st year. Application opens early May
https://www.tylenol.com/sites/tylenol_us/
files/2018-19_tylenol_future_care_scholarship_faq.pdf

PEO Scholar Awards
The P.E.O. Scholar Awards are one-time, competitive, merit-based awards intended to recognize and encourage academic excellence and achievement by women in doctoral-level programs. These awards provide partial support for study and research.

P.E.O. Scholars have demonstrated their ability to make significant contributions in their chosen field of study, having assumed leadership positions in university academics, scientific research, medicine, law, performing arts, international economics, history, literature, government and other demanding fields.

https://www.peointernational.org/about-peo-scholar-awards (more specific site)

http://www.peointernational.org/peo-projects-and-philanthropies

Ryu Family Foundation
Seol Bong Scholarship is available to U.S. Citizens or permanent residents of Korean ancestry who are legal residents and pursuing an advanced degree in one of the following states: CT, DE, ME, MA, NH, NJ, NY, PA, RI, or VT. Minimum GPA of 3.5. Formal application, essay, transcripts and recommendations due by October 1. http://www.ryufoundation.org/

American Medical Women's Association (AMWA)
AMWA awards 4 (four) $1000 scholarships to women currently enrolled in medical school. Awardees will be chosen based on the embodiment of the goals of AMWA. Financial need, though not a requirement, is also considered. Applications are accepted during two periods of the academic year: August 1-September 30 and November 1-December 15. Please submit applications only during the listed periods. For more information please visit website. More resources for women.
https://www.amwa-doc.org/students/awards/medical-education-scholarship/

Anne C. Carter Global Health Fellowship
American Medical Women's Association (AMWA) honors the memory of Anne

C. Carter, MD, with an annual award for outstanding student leadership. The recipient will receive $1000, and the nominating chapter, if applicable, will also receive $1000. The annual nomination deadline is October 1. Must be in AMWA club to be nominated.

https://www.amwa-doc.org/doctors/awards-for-physicians/anne-c-carter/

American Business Women's Association (ABWA) Foundation

Scholarships and loans are offered by ABWA through the Stephen Bufton Memorial Fund. Scholarships range from $3,000 to $10,000. Candidates for special scholarships need not be sponsored by a chapter and information about the scholarship is mailed to designated universities each year. Unsure what deadline.

https://sbmef.org/

Scholarship during MS 3

https://www.aamc.org/initiatives/awards/nickens-student/

These awards consist of five scholarships given to outstanding students entering their third year of medical school who have shown leadership in efforts to eliminate inequities in medical education and health care and have demonstrated leadership efforts in addressing educational, societal, and health care needs of racial and ethnic minorities in the *United States*. Each recipient receives a $5,000 scholarship

American Medical Association (AMA) Physicians of Tomorrow Award

These $10,000 scholarships reward current third-year medical students/individuals who are approaching their final year of medical school. The number of recipients is determined after all applications have been received. Typically, 8-12 recipients in total are selected. Each medical school can nominate one person for each of the different scholarship opportunities (2 nominees in total). Each scholarship category takes into consideration academic excellence and financial need. Each $10,000 scholarship is based on different eligibility requirements
http://www.ama-assn.org/ama/pub/about-ama/ama-foundation/our-programs/medicaleducation/physicians-tomorrow-scholarships.page

Links to More Scholarships

Brown Medical School: https://www.brown.edu/academics/

medical/financial-aid/scholarships

From University of Colorado Medical School: http://www.ucdenver.edu/academics/colleges/medicalschool/education/studentaffairs/studentresources/Documents/External%20Scholarship%20Opportunities.pdf

From University of Minnesota Medical School: https://www.med.umn.edu/sites/med.umn.edu/files/financial-aid-supplemental-scholarship-booklet-2017.pdf

CHAPTER 10:
GAP YEAR

Gap year Strategy

The bulk of this section is to discuss why a gap year was beneficial for my application and wellbeing. According to AAMC, approximately 60% of matriculating medical students took at least 1 gap year between their college graduation and medical school matriculation[19.] I have also heard personal stories from students that many first year medical students (that did not take a gap year after college graduation) are beginning to take time off after their first year of medical school because they are being burned out – and it makes sense. The process of getting into college and medical school are becoming increasingly competitive. Students are preparing their journey by being heavily involved in their high school years so they have the opportunity to attend a competitive undergraduate institution. Most competitive students probably took multiple Honors and AP courses during high school and began immersing themselves in community service activities "to look good on their resume." Student's stress and anxiety levels are probably doubled during their undergraduate years due to the fear of being "weeded out" from premed courses. At the same time, they are scheduling to attend office hours so they can establish good relationships with their professors in hopes that they will write you a good letter of recommendation. Students will most likely immerse in research projects, volunteer activities, extra-curricular activities, and medical brigade trips on top of their academic studies. With medical school applicants becoming more competitive every year, it makes sense that admissions will most likely admit those who are well-rounded in EVERY SINGLE CATEGORY. It is no wonder why students are being burned out by the end of their senior year.

♠ I feel a need to take a moment and stop my writing right here. There are probably a lot of various emotions that readers (assuming you are a student) are feeling right now. Let's see if you fall into any of these 3 categories:

Type 1: You are absolutely agreeing with what I have just said because you are currently overwhelmed. You realized everything you have done and while you are proud of yourself, you aren't sure if you can do more at this point. Congrats on your achievements thus far, and take a break.

Type 2: You didn't realize how overwhelmed you were because you were always "go-go-go." You didn't have a chance to sit back and relax because you always thought about what you needed to accomplish tomorrow, next week, and next year. After reading this paragraph, you realized that you have accomplished a lot of things and it might be worthwhile to take a break.

Type 3: This is the most dangerous group of students that I would like to describe. You have done all the activities you needed to do to become a successful medical school applicant. You know you are qualified and you understand all the things that I have just said, however, you do not think that this pertains to you. You think "ah, I know a lot of friends who are experiencing burn out, but that will never happen to me." If you are feeling this way, please stop, and get to know yourself and your emotions.

♠ Of course, I'm not saying that people must take a gap year because they will get burned out. I am explaining that it is worthwhile to reflect on yourself. No matter what "type of student you are," it is crucial that you know yourself and understand your limits. I believe that it is better to recognize that you are becoming overwhelmed and plan your course of action accordingly rather than realizing too late that you are already burned out..

♠ It is easy to understand how burnout and academic exhaustion can negatively impact your happiness, health, academics, and relationships. However, the hardest part is understanding your limits in an objective way. Some initial warning signs of burnout may include fatigue, lack of motivation, frustration, decreased performance, relationship problems, mental exhaustion, or prolonged unhappiness. If you notice these signs, it is crucial to take a step back.

Overall, I believe that taking a gap year has been an incredible experience for me. To be honest, I thought my gap year would be filled with travel, sky diving, and once in a lifetime opportunities. However, so far, my gap year has been filled with tutoring students, working as a medical scribe, hanging out with friends, playing tennis, eating Korean food, and sleeping. I originally thought that I was wasting my gap year because I wasn't doing anything exciting or exotic. However, I soon realized how beneficial this gap year has been to my self-growth, self-discovery, and wellbeing. I remember being pretty exhausted at the end of my senior year and I cannot imagine starting medical school without taking a gap year. It's also weird thinking that this was my first significant break since I had started school in Preschool! Overall, I believe that my gap year has prepared me for medical school and I am excited to start studying again.
P.S. Since I left home at the age of 15 to attend a residential high school, it has been nice spending more time with my parents and family.

If you are struggling to figure out whether you should take a gap year or not, I encourage you to speak with your prehealth adviser, parents, and peers. More and more students are taking a gap year before starting medical school and the stigmatism of taking a year off is surely decreasing. If you are afraid of taking a gap year because your "parents will be disappointed," then I encourage you to sit down with your family to discuss your point of view and allow them to understand what you can gain from taking a year off. I believe that it's perfectly fine to say that you are exhausted from schooling and you think it will be beneficial to start medical school with a fresh mind. Ultimately, this is your life and you are the one going to medical school – not your parents. I have spoken to many of my medical school friends who decided to attend medical school right after college and most of them, if not all, have told me how taking a break of school would have positively helped them.

That being said, it would be incorrect to say that you can "just rest" during your gap year. When applying to medical schools, many of them ask what you have done during your gap year. This means that you still have to be preoccupied and should be doing something to improve yourself. Whether it's a clinical job or a job that you think will bring positive energy into your life, immerse in it! Unfortunately, playing video games will not be an acceptable answer.

Altogether, I believe that a Gap Year is extremely useful and something that my pre-health adviser advocated for numerous reasons. Here are 10 reasons why the Northwestern Pre-health advisers recommend students to consider a gap year[20]:

1. Flexibility with MCAT

It is already difficult to balance school, extracurricular activities, and volunteering experiences. Imagine taking the MCAT in the middle of these commitments. Taking a gap year means you will have more flexibility in terms of studying for the MCAT and applying to medical school. A gap year will also allow you to focus on preparing for the MCAT more thoroughly.

2. Flexibility with Medical School Applications

Medical school applications include sending transcripts,

gathering letter of recommendations, taking the MCAT, research schools to apply, writing the primary statement, writing secondary statements, and attending interviews. Taking a gap year means you can start preparing these materials earlier.

In my case, I was able to graduate a semester earlier. This allowed me to focus on my application without balancing academics and other school commitments.

3. Improve GPA

Applying directly to medical school without taking a gap year means that your cumulative and science GPA will only be comprised of courses up until your junior year. Since premed courses often "weed out" students, it will be more difficult to secure a good grade during your freshman and sophomore years. Therefore, students often do better in their junior and senior years. With a gap year, you will be able to include your senior year grades which will most likely enhance your GPA. Additionally, taking a gap year will allow you to solely focus on the GPA while attending school without having to prepare for applications or miss classes due to interviews.

4. Enhance community and clinical experiences

Many students often lack sufficient community service experiences or clinical observation hours. Therefore, a gap year will allow you to gain more experiences under your belt. You will gain a better understanding about the field of medicine which will help you answer the "Why Medicine" question during secondary applications and interviews.

5. It is inevitable that students with more experiences will be more competitive applicants.

Admissions committees have acknowledged that younger applicants "suffer by comparison" to an older applicant who hold more awards and experiences under their belt such as research publications, clinical experiences, complete academic history, etc. It is a no brainer that someone with more experiences will win this competition.

6. Better Letters of Recommendations

Spending more time and building better relationships with potential recommenders will generate stronger letters. For example, I was able to receive a letter from a physician because I became a medical scribe.

7. Financial Benefits

Applying to medical school is expensive. I spent over $13,000 over my entire application process including MCAT materials, MCAT exam fee, application payments, interview travel costs, etc. Therefore, working for 1 year can help repay any student loans while also paying for the application process. Remember, the more school you apply to, the more expensive the entire process will be.

8. Gap year is gaining popularity

According to the prehealth advisor, more than 70% of Northwestern students who are accepted to medical school are taking time off after graduation. Many students state that they have found something productive to do during their gap year. Perhaps the reason why a gap year is gaining popularity amongst students and being more attractive to admissions committees is because of the new experiences and perspectives students bring to class, as well as the maturity gained throughout these experiences.

9. Life is Short!

Perhaps there is an interest you always wanted to pursue. I

believe that it will be more difficult to pursue these interests during medical school and after graduation due to financial reasons, family obligations, and a professional schedule. Now is the time to pursue something you've always wanted to do!

10.   Allow your brain to take a break

I believe this is my biggest reason that students should take a gap year. Undergraduate academics are rigorous and medical school will be filled with even more obligations and responsibilities. Therefore, taking a break for the first time in 18 years is something that is extremely appropriate and something you should consider doing! This will also help you from experiencing burn out as a medical school student[20].

Adapted from Northwestern HPA Gap Year. Northwestern University HPA. (n.d.).

What Should I do During my Gap Year

Prior to taking my gap year, I wasn't quite sure what I wanted to do. After a quick research and speaking to my prehealth adviser, I saw that most premed students were either involved with EMT, medical scribe, or research experiences. For a long time I continued to ask people about their experiences and wasn't quite sure what job would be best during my gap year. Here were my thoughts for each activity:

EMT: EMT would allow direct patient care. However, I wasn't sure how I felt about driving the ambulance truck or becoming a technician in the hospital. I had done plenty of emergency department volunteering which included cleaning bedrooms, transporting patients, and restocking rooms. While technicians could care for patients, do EKGs, and perform other basic procedures, I saw that many technicians were spending their time cleaning bedrooms and transporting patients. I wanted to learn more about medical terminologies and understand how providers diagnose patients. Therefore, since most EMT's leave the patient's room once the providers arrive, I knew I wouldn't be able to observe any patient-physician interaction as an EMT. In addition, I needed to take extra courses to become EMT-certified. I wasn't too ecstatic about paying money to take more courses to become an EMT.

Basic Science Research: I was also interested in continuing my research from my undergraduate institution; however, I felt that I had enough research experiences already that I was looking for a change. I was in need of more clinical experiences in my application (and definitely not research experience) that I was leaning towards becoming an EMT or medical scribe. However, for those that do not have research experience, or are looking to apply to a MD/PHD program, I encourage you to gain additional research experiences!

Medical Scribe: I was most interested in becoming a medical scribe because scribes went into patient rooms with the providers. This would allow me to listen to the patient's narratives and also observe how the providers (physicians, physician assistants, and nurse practitioners) diagnose and care for patients. Although my job would be spent typing on a computer, I loved the idea that I could see all the cases from start to finish. In the end, I decided to become a medical scribe. It has been an incredible experience because I am exposed to many different patient cases and have the opportunity to learn medical terminologies. Furthermore, since I work directly with the providers, I was able to establish relationships with them and ask for letter of recommendations.

Alternative Gap Year Opportunities
Clinical or Public Health Research: Most premed students will likely have basic science research experiences. If you don't want to continue your undergraduate research and are thinking about clinical research, this would be the way to go. Also, it is much easier to publish clinical research materials than basic

science research. Therefore, if you are able to spend one year and publish your research, then this will be extremely advantageous when applying to medical school.

Teach for America: Teaching as a part of Teach for America program will look extremely favorable on your application. Joining Teach for America is very competitive and is a 2 year commitment. Therefore, those looking to take only one gap year will not be able to apply to this program.

Healthcare Consultant: Undergraduate students with often an economic, accounting, or financial major who are interested in the medical field may apply to become a healthcare consultant. This is a division of consulting that requires you to understand health systems well. Becoming a consultant during your gap year will probably allow you to make the most money (compared to other gap year experiences). Although there are no clinical experiences with this opportunity, you will gain a comprehensive understanding about healthcare from a systems perspective.

Advanced Degrees (MPH, MPP, MBA's): Students who would like a master's degree prior to attending medical school can apply to 1-2 year master programs to make yourself a more competitive applicant. If you are looking to apply to a MD/Ph.D program, a master's degree may be more useful to your application. Since I was certain that I was not going to apply to a MD/Ph.D program, I thought a master's was not useful for my career and definitely not worth my money.

Post-Bacc Program: I believe that the Post-Bacc program will be advantageous only for two types of students. Those that wish to increase their GPA (record enhancers), and those who need to complete premed course requirements after they graduated from college (career change). There are some Post-Bacc Programs that have a strong relationship with medical schools. These linkage programs allow either a guaranteed admission into their medical school or a guaranteed interview offer as long as you maintain a certain GPA and MCAT score. Therefore, if you choose to do a Post-Bacc, then consider choosing a program that increases your odds of getting into the medical school. Speak to your pre-health adviser whether or not you should enroll in a Post-Bacc program due to a low GPA. AAMC published a Postbaccalaureate pre-medical program database that offers all Post-Bacc programs: https://apps.aamc.org/post-bac/#/index

Non-Medical Job: Although some students choose to do a non-medical job for their gap year experience, I believe that this is a very risky decision. Unless this non-medical job is unique such as starting a company, becoming a professional sports player/ musician, or joining the army, I believe that most non-medical jobs will not be drastically advantageous to your application. Although medical school admissions state that they are moving towards a more holistic review of a student's application, a student must be able to showcase their passion for medicine. For this purpose, I believe it will be much easier to showcase their interest and commitment in medicine by involving in clinical experiences during their gap year.

Personal Reflection:

After deliberating on my choices, I decided to return to my hometown and become an Emergency Department medical scribe. Since I left home to go a residential high school, I realized that I hadn't spent time with my parents since when I was 15 years old. Therefore, I was excited to return home to join my parents (& most definitely save money on rent). In addition to becoming a full-time medical scribe, I became a part-time virtual tutor for LanguageWill, a counseling service company located in Seoul, South Korea. Through this company, I tutored students in SAT, ACT, AP, and IB standardized testing. I also decided to become a volunteer for the Peoria Rescue Ministries to educate women on basic computer education.

In addition to my activities and commitments, I involved myself in the things that have always given me happiness: tennis! I remember playing competitively during high school and wanted to experience the joy that I gained from playing this sport. Since I am not a big fan of working out, playing tennis has been fulfilling my exercise needs. I hope to continue to play tennis while in medical school.

Altogether, my gap year experience has been pleasant and fulfilling. I've been spending time my family, growing my faith, understanding who I am, maintaining my wellbeing, playing tennis, and catching up on my long lost sleep. I've also spent my gap year traveling to South Korea to see my grandparents and going to Guatemala for the first time as a part of the medical missions trip. Most importantly, I enjoy how much I have grown as a person and matured over the year. I believe that my gap year experience will allow me to become a better medical student and a better physician. I would most definitely recommend every student to take a gap year and take a moment to recognize how fast their life has been passing before their eyes.

CHAPTER 11: BUILDING YOUR MEDICAL SCHOOL LIST

I remember feeling especially overwhelmed right before my medical school list. I bought the AAMC MSAR (Medical School Admission Requirements) online resource that YOU MUST BUY. This resource shows all the different MD medical schools and their descriptions. I remember going through the entire MSAR list and writing down schools that either sounded familiar or I thought would be a potential school. At the end of my list, there were about 60 medical schools! However, I could easily delete some schools after doing some research. In the end, I decided to apply to 40 schools. I know this sounds a lot (and it is a lot!!); however, I didn't want to regret not applying to any schools that I wanted to. In this section, I would like to discuss how I chose my 40 MD school. There are currently about 141 Allopathic programs and 34 Osteopathic programs in the US[4].

I first encourage you to buy the MSAR resource that is the official medical school resource coming from the official AAMC website. It sells for $28.00 and it will provide you with the resources for exactly 1 year. You can go to this URL: https://store.aamc.org/medical-school-admission-requirements-msar-for-u-s-and-canadian-medical-schools-online.html.

If you are thinking about applying DO schools, you could take a look at the official collection book from AACOM which is free: https://www.aacom.org/become-a-doctor/us-coms

Since I bought MSAR in November 2017 (which I would say is pretty early to buy), I had to renew the subscription for an additional year so I could continue to have the resource throughout my 2019 cycle application process. With the MSAR website opened, I created a google excel spreadsheet of all the different factors that I considered important. Therefore, I encourage you to also create some kind of organizational method before building your medical school list. Of course, it will be exceptionally helpful to know your cumulative GPA, science GPA, and MCAT score.

Filter by MCAT Scores

While medical school admissions are transitioning into a "holistic review" admissions process, this is without saying that MCAT still remains to be an important factor into medical school admissions. Therefore, it is important that you are realistic in your search. For example, it will be nearly impossible to gain admissions into a medical school with an average MCAT score of 520 if you only have a 510 (unless you have some kind of outstanding factor to consider for). In my experience, I gained the most interview invitations from schools that were either equal or lower than my MCAT. The graph below shows the number of medical schools with its average MCAT scores that I applied to. The green bars represent the number of interview invitations I received from medical schools with its respective average MCAT scores. Overall, I found the most success from applying to medical schools that had a similar or lower MCAT score as me. Remember, I received a composite score of 512.

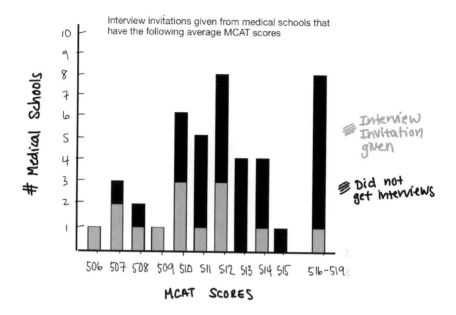

Interview invitations given from medical schools that have the following average MCAT scores

Medical Schools (y-axis)

MCAT SCORES (x-axis): 506 507 508 509 510 511 512 513 514 515 516-519

Interview Invitation given

Did not get interviews

Public vs. Private Medical School

Check which schools are public or private on MSAR. Private schools do not care if you are an IS (In-state) or OOS (Out-of-State) applicant. Many public schools prefer those who have IS ties. There are some schools that place significance of IS ties over others. For example, University of Colorado have a higher percentage of selection OOS applicants compared to many California public schools. If you are applying to a OOS public school, then ask yourself if you can write about any ties to that particular area. Many schools ask about any family connections – this would be the perfect place to talk about your family "legacies."

♠ To increase your chances of acceptance, apply to all medical schools in your state of residency including private and public schools. Some states have more medical schools than others. For example, there are 7 MD medical schools in Illinois compared to only 1 MD medical school in Colorado.

Prerequisites

There are some medical schools that are very strict in their prerequisite requirements while other medical schools have become competency-based admissions. Most schools recommend applicants to complete 1 year of biology, 1 year of physics, 1 year of English, 1 year of chemistry (biochemistry may be included in chemistry requirement), and 1 year of organic chemistry. However, I also recommend students to take a Psychology course and a Sociology course because it shows up on your MCAT. MSAR lists all the required/recommended course work.

♠ Your undergraduate prehealth department is likely to list the premed course list. As long as you take your college's premed track courses, I don't think you have anything to worry about.

Recommendation Letter Requirements

Look up the recommendation letter requirements for each medical school by looking it up on their websites. Some medical schools such as the New York Medical College requires a "non-science professor" recommendation letter. Since I did not have a non-science professor recommendation letter, I could not apply to all medical schools that had this requirement. Most medical schools usually recommend a non-science professor. Remember, if it is a recommendation, you may still apply to the school even if you don't have that particular letter.

Additionally, medical schools sometimes differentiate between the word "faculty" and "professor." Faculty is an umbrella term that includes professor. However, if they require a "professor" letter, then it has to be your professor who gave you an academic grade. In this case, a graduate TA or a post-doc member cannot write the letter for you. On the other hand, if the school asks for a "faculty" member, then a TA or an alternative school staff member is appropriate.

♠ Refer to the recommendation letter chapter to learn more about tips/advices on how to build your list of recommendation letters.

Placement History such as HBCU

HBCU stands for Historically Black Colleges and Universities which was originally founded to educate students of African-American decent. There are 4 noteworthy medical schools that are considered HBCUs, and statistically have a higher matriculation of those that have a Race & Ethnicity of Black or from an African American decent. These include the following:

Howard University College of Medicine
Charles R. Drew University of Medicine and Science
MeHarry Medical College
Morehouse School of Medicine

Primary Care Focus vs. Research Focus
There are clearly medical schools that have a higher research focus than others. Although there are no schools that require applicants to have research experiences, if you do not have any research experiences, then consider applying to medical schools that place less emphasis on research. Check out the mission statement of each school to see their specific emphasis and values. If a particular medical school requires all medical students to perform research, then it's clearly obvious that admissions will expect applicants to have research experience.

Geographical Location
If I was asked the question "Where do you want to go?," I often said "anywhere that will take me." While this would have been the case if I was accepted to one place, I believe that going to a place you are comfortable is crucial and will play a factor into your happiness.
Ask yourself these questions before you apply or during your interview date:
Do you feel comfortable going to that location?
Do you have a preference on Rural, Suburb, or Urban locations & the # of population?
Do you need to be close to family?
Does weather play a huge factor into your happiness?

Cost
All medical schools vary in their tuition, fees, and cost of living. You can check out the cost of each medical school in MSAR.

Curriculum
While I believe that all medical school will give you an excellent education, schools vary in their grading system and teaching methodology. Some schools are pass/fail while others have a more traditional grading system. Some schools are strictly PBL (problem based learning), while others have a more traditional lecture based curriculum. Some schools have an organized pathway set in place, while other schools have a list of electives you can choose from. It will be strategic to go to a medical school that has a curriculum that is structured in a way that you learn best.

Residency Placement
Although this information will not be available to you on MSAR, most schools release this information on their website. Check our their average USMLE test scores and residency placement. Some schools will place a large number of their students in the same state, while other resident placements will be more dispersed across the United States.

CHAPTER 12: ESSAY COLLECTIONS

Primary Statement

Writing the primary statement will be one of the most difficult components in your application process. As a pre-med student, you were told a list of "to-do" items that needed to be completed in order to apply to medical schools such as having research experience, completing pre-med courses, volunteering in hospitals, and amassing hundreds of community service hours. Whether you volunteered in your local church or medical clinic due to some internal motivation, or a means to check off this to-do list, it will be much harder to merely "check things off" when writing a personal statement. When pre-med students began writing their application essays, they forget the many intangible qualities they possess. Rather than making themselves come to life on paper by showcasing their personal narrative, pre-meds do what they do best by listing their academic awards, accomplishments, and service. Therefore, writing an impactful personal essay will be as foreign to pre-meds as procrastination and last-minute studying. :)

Every admissions officer understands that we are not professional writers. They do not expect us to create an elegant work of art featuring the complexity of our lives through mystery and foreshadow. I can assure you that they would rather appreciate a straight-forward story of our initial motivation and commitment to medicine. If you are able to include the critical components of the personal statement such as your initial motivation to medicine, commitment to medicine, and confirmation of your interest in medicine, then you can still produce an impactful personal statement, even if your writing is average.

Since I knew that I would have difficulty writing my essays, I decided to enroll in the Princeton Review Medical School Admissions counseling which was $2,500. With this program, I would have an adviser who would proofread my primary statement, work&activities, and secondary essays. While I believe that the price of this package is overpriced, I do think that it was helpful in many ways. (I will discuss more later)

In this section, I will share my progression of the primary essay that I wrote for my medical school application. I wrote about 9 drafts before I decided that it was appropriate and good enough to submit it. Interestingly, I made about 3-4 drafts from scratch before I stuck with my final draft. After each draft, I submitted it to either my Northwestern pre-med health adviser or my Princeton Review adviser (yes, I decided to enroll in the PR medical school consulting) and made reviews based on their feedback. I will copy and paste my drafts and also post the feedback I had on my essay. By reading the progression of my essays, I hope these will be able to help you on your primary statement! P.S. I did not focus on my grammar when working on my drafts, please forgive my grammatical errors.

♠ Note, I wrote 9 drafts before I submitted my final version of the personal statement. However, I will only include the essays where I made significant changes. Notice the progression of my ideas throughout my drafts. In my beginning drafts, I ran into the trap of merely listed my activities, experiences, and accomplishments (something may premeds will do on their first draft). Pay close attention to how I was able to transform my activities and competencies into an emotional story of how I was able to confirm my motivation to pursue medicine.

After writing multiple personal statement drafts and listening to the feedback from my advisers, I realized that the personal statement must include these 3 critical components:

1. Describe your initial interest & motivation for pursuing medicine.
2. Show how you continued to pursue medicine
3. Show how you confirmed your interests in medicine and why you will be an effective physician

Before drafting your personal statement, ask yourself these questions[21]:

1. Am I explaining my passion of medicine and ways of confirming my motivation?
2. Am I explaining "why medical school?"
3. Am I articulating or showing my competencies?
4. Do I have an overarching theme, flow, and transitions?

Personal Statement Draft 1

We forget those that are misfortunate enough to fall through the cracks of our system. This system of legislation and order are often praised for what perceives to be an all-encompassing foundation in which all individuals may exist in harmony and equality. Inarguably, with the complexity of human existence, the minorities are bound to become unapologetically behind and forgotten.

*This would be an appropriate introduction of a theory paper. The point of the personal statement is to be genuine and connect with readers. This paragraph does not fulfill that.

This imperfect system was officially acknowledged at 17 years of age when I constructed and lead a team of high school students to present a K-12 school funding initiative to Illinois state senators and lobbyists. With an early passion of tutoring the underserved population, I was armed with past experiences, objective knowledge, and maturity to lead an education reform. I recalled the wide disparities in educational expenditures in the state of Illinois and offered a case of five intricately designed formulas dedicated in closing wide education disparities amongst students and in saving those who had drowned through the cracks of the old education system. Although my ideas were later dismissed, I recognized the power, inspiration, and impact I brought to my community in creating positive social change.

*This has nothing to do with your passion in medicine. This also does not recognize your motivations to pursue medicine. Although you state a passion of yours, this paragraph would be more appropriate in your Work&Activities section.

I continued to foster my passion in creating a social impact by becoming the president of a mentorship program called Illuminate at my university. Illuminate shares my values of serving those underserved by providing academic assistance to underprivileged perspective first-generation college students. Through this program, I had the honor of mentoring a girl who lacked self-confidence and self-worth. To her, "nothing in life seem[ed] to work" and her dreary eyes displayed the exhaustion of her family and financial circumstances. She was convinced that her dream of attending college was too farfetched. Determined to seize this opportunity, I was motivated to build a personal relationship to discern her strengths and construct an individualized model for her academic success.

*This is objectifying and making her "into a project to seize this opportunity." Do not write "seize this opportunity" because it sounds like a business language. Rather, describe how you individualized the program. Did you explain things in a different way? How were you able to discern her strengths? Were you able to have the flexibility to adjust and present those ideas in a different way? Doctors must use adaptability and flexibility because all patients are different. Doctors need these characteristics to connect with patients and guide patients to their understanding. Therefore, highlight the importance of understanding as this directly correlates to their comfort.

One special night, I picked up a phone call only to hear deadly piercing screams of joy and disbelief that she was accepted to college. Interestingly, what made this moment the most influential and memorable was neither her appreciation nor her acceptance, but the mere idea that my time and presence had the capacity to permanently change her future. I grasped the power of using relationships to improve the lives of others. She was no longer forgotten, and she had rose from the cracks of the system.

*This paragraph seems too dramatic, too farfetched, and reflects your glory. Know when to give glory to others and when to focus on yourself.

Due to moments like these, I am often asked and encouraged to become a teacher. However, my aspiration is to become a physician because while enhancing the quality of life through educational social change is important, I am convinced that the most fundamental level of quality of life is via the rejuvenation of health. I have endlessly witnessed that the enhancement of life cannot commence until health is restored. Therefore, as a physician has only the means to offer this service, I am passionate and committed in becoming a physician.

*It is understood that this paragraph was a method for you to connect your passion of teaching to medicine. However, this does not show why you want to become a physician. Suddenly plugging in this paragraph will not answer the question "Why Medicine."

*Furthermore, you do not mention health until now. You need to show how you truly internalized the decision to pursue medicine and show how you stepped out of your boundry to confirm your interests in medicine.

To wholeheartedly witness and experience the act of becoming of service to those in need, I became the vice-president of the Medlife chapter at my university to organize and lead medical mission trips in Cusco, Peru. In the hilly outskirts of Cusco, mothers carrying children continued to hike for miles in hopes that our mobile clinic physicians would examine them. In the midst of assisting physicians and dentists with procedures, I vastly noticed what looked like a man struggling to walk from afar. I quickly set my instruments down and sprinted towards him. When I finally reached his destination, my eyes caught his discolored body and tightly wrapped ankles. Quickly assisting him back to the mobile clinic and apologetically convincing patients already in line of his urgency, I gently laid him on the table on behalf of the physician. What I witnessed next was unfathomable. As the doctor carefully unraveled the dirty blood stained wrap, I startled, when bone was exposed. A bacterial infection had eaten its way through the flesh. As my heart and jaw dropped, I was overwhelmed by his misfortune. A simple pill of antibiotics could have saved this preventable disease; yet this man was merely ecstatic to live at all. At this moment, his beaming smile allowed me to witness the beauty of medically serving others as it transcended all cultural and linguistic barriers. Nevertheless, through the lens of providing free healthcare to the underserved population in Cusco, educating families about preventative care, communicating compassion and concern for their welfare, I confirmed my passion and commitment of becoming a physician.

*This serves nothing except to describe a story of tragedy. You can use this example; however, you need to write more about your traits, how you articulated your competencies, and what you noticed about physicians to confirm your desire to go to medical school. Why would you be a good fit for a medical school to accept you?

Currently, I am a full time medical scribe in the ER department while also continuing my passion of increasing the quality of life of those homeless in my community by leading preventative care education and measuring blood pressure. A simple "Oh, yes I needed my blood pressure to be taken" gives me a sense of fulfillment for playing an integral role in the care of my community members. I have now established a deep personal connection with these members at the Peoria Rescue Ministries as I continue to my interest for education by tutoring them in GED (General Equivalency Development) coursework and basic computer skills. By encouraging and motivating these individuals to regularly exercise and stick to a healthy diet while enhancing their academic education, I have successfully confirmed my desire and dedication as a physician also teaching in medical education.

Understanding the rigors in the preparation of a physician, I have maintained strong time-management skills and work ethics by successfully balancing my service-oriented lifestyle in addition to my strong academic and research endeavors that fosters my analytic nature. A prominent physician demonstrates high aptitudes in service orientation, social skills, cultural competencies, and leadership. I am confident that my comprehensive set of skills obtained via social change and clinical experiences have provided invaluable lessons in all areas. I believe that a medical education will provide me with the educational principles essential in cultivating and enhancing the lives of those in need.

*The last 2 paragraphs are more of what should be included in your essay because it shows how you are immersing yourself to help others and learn more about medicine.

*Overall, this essay does not show the progression of your interest to medicine. You talk about your passion of teaching (which a fine topic to write about), but it is not well orchestrated with your passion in medicine. You need to talk more about why medicine, why you are drawn into medicine, and how you confirmed that. This essay is too much on wanting to help people, and consequently, you don't share about your complete motivation for medicine. Frankly, this essay seems would be perfect if you were applying to become a teacher or a social worker.

*Note, it is perfectly okay to talk about your other non-medical interests or passion as long as you can weave it into why you are wanting to pursue medicine. Unfortunately, although you try to weave in your passion of teaching and medicine together, it was incoherent.

*Always keep in mind that you can write about your specific activities and experiences in the Work&Actvities section. Therefore, do not think that you need to include all your experiences in your personal statement.

Personal Statement Draft 2

The quality of life cannot commence until health is restored. Life in the modern day is fast and our perspective of time has never been faster –except when health is threatened and life unexpectedly halts. During this stage, panic overrides as all feelings of uncertainty and vulnerability rapidly replace security and predictability. Meanwhile, time continues to tick for others, and we often overlook patients' personal comfort and security.

*Again, the introduction seems like the introduction of an academic paper. I see that you're trying to engage the reader but try to break this habit. Perhaps you write these kinds of introduction because you have always written academic papers.

*The introducing tone is negative because you describe a negative perspective about medicine. Although overlooking patient's comfort and security is a true problem in medicine, we don't have to know facts about what is going on in medicine – we should rather, talk about our own experiences in medicine. You don't need to try to explain something that the admissions officers already know.

I first recognized this ideation in the form of education. Academic institutions enforcing an education system for the mass inevitably results in de-individualization. Students fallen through the cracks are unapologetically behind and forgotten. These students, like patients, are stricken with panic and apprehension. So with my passion for service, I helped create Illuminate, a personalized mentorship program catered to revive these students.

Through the mentorship program, I was immediately distraught when the grades of my mentee Anna did not flourish. My profound set of teaching skills and confidence in tutoring was not enough. However, with the flexibility and adaptability to adjust, I changed the curriculum for our next meeting: we were just going to talk. The next hour became the most fruitful and eye-opening experience. Anna had an incredible talent of writing poems that she used as an outlet throughout difficult life circumstances. When I creatively took her inherent thinking process and adapted it to her academic coursework, Anna's problem solving and self-confidence fostered. By building a personal relationship, I had the opportunity to understand her life circumstances, apply that to discover her strengths, and acquire adaptability to communicate ideas that reflected her strengths.

*What does the Illuminate mentorship program have to do with you being a doctor? Unless you talk about how education is crucial with a patient in order to create a physician-patient interaction, I believe that this activity belongs in the Work&Activities section.

Due to these moments, I was often asked and encouraged to become a teacher. While I believe enhancing the quality of life through educational social change is important, I am convinced that the most fundamental level of quality of life is through the rejuvenation of health. The greatest gift of a physician is becoming an integrative part of the most vulnerable state of a patient. With my desire to serve others in their greatest time of need, and equipped with creativity and flexibility to communicate ideas differently, my passion and commitment in securing the health of patients as a future physician blossomed.

To wholeheartedly witness and experience the act of becoming of service to those in need, I became the vice-president of the Medlife chapter at my university to organize and lead medical mission trips in Cusco, Peru. In the hilly outskirts of Cusco, mothers carrying children continued to hike for miles in hopes that our mobile clinic physicians would examine them. In the midst of assisting physicians and dentists with procedures, I vastly noticed what looked like a man struggling to walk from afar. I quickly set my instruments down and sprinted towards him. When I finally reached his destination, my eyes caught his discolored body and tightly wrapped ankles. Quickly assisting him back to the mobile clinic and apologetically convincing patients already in line of his urgency, I gently laid him on the table on behalf of the physician. What I witnessed next was unfathomable. As the doctor carefully unraveled the dirty blood stained wrap, I startled, when bone was exposed. A bacterial infection had eaten its way through the flesh. As my heart and jaw dropped, I was overwhelmed by his misfortune. A simple pill of antibiotics could have saved this preventable disease; yet this man was merely ecstatic to live at all. At this moment, his beaming smile allowed me to witness the beauty of medically serving others as it transcended all cultural and linguistic barriers. Nevertheless, through the lens of providing free healthcare to the underserved population in Cusco, educating families about preventative care, communicating compassion and concern for their welfare, I confirmed my passion and commitment of becoming a physician.

*Please refer to my feedback from draft 1. If you want to use the Peru experience, you must talk more about what your reflections and what you observed. Did you recognize any limitations? Do you think that preventative medicine is important? Perhaps this example is more appropriate in the Works&Activities section or your secondary essays.

I continued to gain direct patient interaction and exposure to health care in the United States by shadowing physicians and volunteering in hospitals; however, I continued to feel limited in my ability to help the patients. One morning while shadowing a cardiovascular surgeon, a Korean woman aged 65 entered the operating room stricken with worry and fear. She could not speak English and I was certain her fear originated from uncertainty and a lack of communication, rather than her upcoming surgery. With permission, I translated what the physician was communicating. Immediately, her eyes widened and displayed signs of relief as she told me in Korean, "I feel safer with you." Although this comment provided me with a great sense of fulfillment for playing an active role during her vulnerable journey, I wished I could do more to improve her health.

*This is a great example. Say more eloquently.

Currently, I became a medical scribe to directly learn what makes a great physician. After working with numerous physicians, I have internalized the difference between physicians who strive to provide sincere compassion, friendliness, and honor toward the patients compared to detached physicians driven to discharge patients. In a time that is extremely fast-paced, we often neglect the vulnerability of patients and forget the importance and power of creating personal relationships. I am confident that my comprehensive set of skills obtained via social change and clinical experiences in addition to a medical education will provide me with the educational principles essential in fully cultivating and enhancing the lives of those in need. As I am convinced that the most fundamental level of quality of life is through the rejuvenation of health, I aspire to become a physician of compassion and sincerity to reestablish communication, comfort, and security to our patients.

*Just talk about the positive qualities of the physician rather than comparing them to a "not so good physician." You can admit that there are limitations of healthcare roles; however, it is difficult to talk about the negative aspects without providing a clear example of a story.

*Quite frankly, your 2nd draft is very similar to your 1st draft. Try to break away from this backbone and create a new draft from scratch. I would like to see what additional you have that are unique to you.

*Themes from this essay: relationships, connection, & individualization

Personal Statement Draft 3

The moment my alarm clock rings, I am cued to make my bed. This small gesture of centering the pillow, pulling the inner sheets taut, and stretching the covers was casted at the age of seven, not to feel organized or responsible, but for the sheer anticipation of jumping back into a made bed. This action that once took considerable effort has now developed into a mundane, but powerful habit that has become the foundation of how I construct a focused (meaningful?) life. From a young age, I understood the importance of valuing the simple tasks in life and created predictive awareness by preparing for delayed gratification.

*Good job not having a "theory introduction." However, "predictive awareness" is difficult to understand. Perhaps you are meaning "mindfulness" or "awareness?" Write in more simple language.

My aspiration is to become a physician because I am convinced that the most fundamental level of quality of life is via the rejuvenation of health. I have endlessly witnessed through familial circumstances, that the enhancement of life cannot commence until health is restored.

My grandfather was diagnosed with Alzheimer's, the slow good-bye disease fifteen years ago. He, an original frontier of South Korean's education system and a talented self-taught artist, was predicted to lose touch with reality more than seven years ago. Therefore, to prolong his neurological functions, I created a personalized preventative curriculum, which included daily physical exercise, chess, painting, puzzles, and memorizing songs. Although he no longer recognizes my presence, I personally witnessed the power of preventative care as it provided five more years of happiness, memory, and the well-being of my grandfather and my family.

*Yes! I see how you were initially drawn to medicine. This is very educational and personalized! I can see a clear connection about how working with your grandfather allowed you to become interested in medicine. A huge part of being a physician is to approach stories that are tailored to each patient.

To confirm my passion for medicine by experiencing healthcare in other parts of the country, I organized a medical mission trip to Cusco, Peru. In the midst of assisting physicians, I had the opportunity to lead a team of volunteers to educate the importance of personal hygiene to young children. Due to the lack of access of toothbrushes, most children lacked complete sets of teeth and some displayed cases of tooth decay that painfully broke through the nerve of the tooth. Luckily, their adult teeth had yet to grow, and I was thrilled to introduce how the beauty of this simple instrument could prevent future devastating oral complications.

My experience at Cusco was two-fold: lack of healthcare makes preventative care difficult and understanding ones culture is critical in implementing optimal treatment options. Before arriving to Peru, I was merely ecstatic to help the community members in any way possible – I was ready to provide a helping hand. Shortly, however, I realized that a toothbrush education was impractical without the viability of toothbrushes. Luckily, toothbrushes that were donated allowed the preservation of oral hygiene for 200 children. Altogether, I witnessed the importance of understanding one's culture and circumstances to accurately diagnose and provide a more comprehensive set of care.

*I like the more general summary of what you experienced while on the brigade trip. However, perhaps this story is more appropriate in the Work&Activities section. It could even be a MME (Most memorable experience) because it shows initiative and the transformative nature of your experience. This characteristic of cultural competency will be fundamental in practicing medicine in a diverse community.

Currently, I am a full time medical scribe in the ER department while also continuing my passion of increasing the quality of life of those homeless in my community by leading preventative care education and measuring blood pressure. A simple "Oh, yes I needed my blood pressure to be taken" gives me a sense of fulfillment for playing an integral role in the care of my community members since I understand the difficulty of access to healthcare in underserved communities.

My childhood core theme of predictive awareness has guided me to instill a better quality of life to others by educating the importance of preventative care and promoting a healthier life. Health is the greatest possession of an individual and becoming an integral part of a family's vulnerable journey in securing their health will give me a sense of reward that no other profession can offer. As a physician has only the means to offer this service, I am passionate and committed in becoming a physician. I am confident that my comprehensive set of skills obtained via social change and clinical experiences have provided invaluable lessons in all areas. I believe that a medical education will provide me with the educational principles essential in cultivating and enhancing the lives of those in need.

*In order for this paragraph to flow better, you should compare how your innate ability as a child to practice something important for you can also be drawn to medicine.

*Themes from this essay: valuing their life, preparing their life, ensuring health, & preparation for future.

Nahee Park Personal Statement Final

He gripped the yellow colored pencil and quietly centered it on the canvas. His scrunched eyebrows and focused eyes signaled diligence as he gently stroked the outline of a yellow tulip. To him, the drawing of a yellow tulip had a remarkable capacity to either empower or depress himself. Petal by petal, his pursed lips gave way to a satisfied grin. I quickly sighed in relief, embracing the optimism that today would be good day.

My grandfather has Alzheimer's, the long goodbye disease. A talented self-taught artist, who once captured majestic sceneries of nature, was predicted to lose touch with reality within seven short years. Determined to prolong his neurological functions, I dove into learning more about the disease. I explored the incorporation of his favorite passions into daily therapeutic routines such as solving puzzles, memorizing songs, and drawing flowers. Over the next years, I learned to adjust this curriculum to incorporate his changing concerns, priorities, and values, which has provided ten more years of happiness. This personal mission, which called for resilience, responsibility, and an exquisite attention to detail, fueled my desire to pursue medicine.

Throughout these interactions with my grandfather, I became fascinated by the human mind and its ability to create consciousness. I desired to learn more. As a medical scribe in the Emergency Department, I am exhilarated by psychiatric cases because they give me an opportunity to apply concepts learned from my undergraduate courses and speculate on the mind's mysteries. From the hundreds of patient interactions I saw, one in particular stood out, not for the diagnosis but rather the physician's display of empathy, compassion, and unique ability to connect with the patient. "Shut the door," the patient hollered with fear stricken across his face as the physician and I walked into the patient's room. Since his arrival, I had sensed his distress as he crouched in the corner and shielded himself with blankets. While I was slightly taken aback by the patient's paranoia, I was inspired by the physician's ability to retain a therapeutic nature by demonstrating deference and thoroughly addressing the patient's emotions and concerns. When his questions heightened the patient's anxieties, the physician calmly alleviated these by asking him about his favorite hobbies and maintained silence as the patient searched for words. The physician approached the case not as a set of symptoms, but the person as a whole, which encouraged the patient to regain eye contact and relay trust. His story began to unfold, which revealed that his visual and auditory hallucinations were creating a notion that someone was out to hurt him. This experience highlighted how sensitivity and compassion underlie human connection, a relationship that must be met before the advancement of any other pursuits. As a medical scribe, I have a responsibility to intently listen to patients and respect their experience by preserving their story in the chart. However, I learned much more than efficient documentation. Just like these physicians, I aspire to become a physician who looks beyond patients' biochemistry and demonstrates compassion to fully advocate and encourage patients to regain their medical agency.

Seeking opportunities to gain additional direct patient interactions, I began shadowing a cardiovascular surgeon, where I had the rare opportunity to serve an integral role in the care of a patient. One morning, an elderly female Korean patient entered the operating room stricken with worry and fear about her five hour open heart surgery. She did not speak English and I sensed that her fear originated from uncertainty and a lack of communication. When the surgeon hurriedly opened Google Translate, I respectfully offered to translate, as I am fluent in Korean. Immediately, the patient's eyes widened and displayed signs of relief as she communicated, "I feel safer with you." Once I realized speaking in native tongue instantly created trust, I continued to reassure her by listening to her concerns. Until the moment of her sedation, I held her hand and prayed for her wellbeing as her calm eyes slipped by. My time as a medical scribe taught me the importance of relaying compassion and earning trust, but this particular experience was monumental because I had a unique opportunity to develop that trust, feel it, and internalize the power of human connection during her most vulnerable times.

When I see yellow tulips, I do not think of the loss and hardships my family endured but of the prevailing cast of hope, perseverance, and fortitude of one's fight for their health. My personal experiences and clinical observations helped me recognize an emotional personal narrative that is a part of every patient. Health is the greatest possession an individual owns and becoming an integral part of a patient's narrative in securing their health will give me a sense of reward that no other profession can offer. I am eager and prepared to deliver culturally competent and sensitive care by integrating my growing educational principles and skills in concert with my concern for others to play a consequential role in helping them draw their own yellow tulip.

♠ Since I saw that my drafts were not making any progression, I decided to take a break for 2 weeks and did not even think about my personal statement. Actually, I was pretty devastated that my advisers were not a fan of my essays so I stopped writing for 2 weeks. After 2 weeks passed, I called my Princeton Review adviser and discussed why things weren't progressing as I thought it would. I remember that she told me that my personal statement did not showcase my personal narrative of my pursuit of medicine. She advised me to write about myself without thinking of impressing the admissions office. After this phone call, I had an epiphany about the general direction of my essay. I went home and wrote this essay in about 2 hours. Surprisingly, rather than fixing my grammar and changing some awkward wordings, the bulk of this essay remained as is. I hope you enjoy reading about my personal narrative and hope that you can learn from my mistakes so you don't waste time creating multiple drafts from scratch. Before you start writing, spend some time brainstorming about your entire life experiences. Don't just think about your recent activities, but go back all the way to your childhood and search for initial influencers or motivators that allowed you to realize your pursuit of medicine.

Although it is easier said than done, don't write for the purposes of impressing the admissions officers. Rather, let the personal statement be an opportunity for you to describe yourself and relay your competencies.

What should I do if I'm also applying to osteopathic schools

The personal essay between allopathic and osteopathic medical schools is similar in that the essay should provide information about why you want to pursue medicine, your commitment to medicine, and why you'll be an effective physician. Due to this profound similarity, most students will initially draft their MD personal essay and then modify this essay to fit the requirements of the DO personal essay. Before drafting the DO personal statement, students should understand the following 2 points.

1. Difference in character count between MD and DO schools

AMCAS (MD Application service) offers 5,300 character count, whereas AACOMAS (DO Application service) offers 4,500 character count limit. Simply shortening the MD personal essay to meet the character count of DO schools is a poor strategy.

2. Don't merely insert cliché phrases such as "holistic," "comprehensive," or "whole-body approach."

Osteopathic admissions committee understand that while there are selected students who are strictly passionate in the osteopathic philosophy, they will know that the majority of pre-med students will apply to osteopathic schools as a form of "safety school" because their average MCAT and GPA scores are lower than MD schools. Therefore, students should not attempt to merely insert words like "holistic approach" or "whole body" to demonstrate their interest in osteopathic medicine. Rather, then shortening your essay and adding clique phrases, students must modify their personal essay to demonstrate why they have a passion in osteopathic medicine. Adding stories and tweaking essays to demonstrate the osteopathic philosophy throughout the essay will be a better approach to modifying your personal statement.

♠ This does not mean to start your DO essay from scratch. My advice for you is to draft your MD personal essay first. Then tweak this essay so it is geared towards more of the osteopathic philosophy. I must admit, I did not make drastic changes on my osteopathic personal essay from my allopathic personal essay. As you see in my "DO Personal Statement" example below, I have kept the overall backbone of my journey to medicine. I was grateful to have been accepted to all 4 osteopathic medical schools with the following essay. However, in order to make your essay more effective and powerful, I advise you to insert more osteopathic driven examples and stories (especially if your MCAT and GPA scores are less competitive).

Nahee Park
Osteopathic Medicine Personal Statement Final

He gripped the yellow colored pencil and quietly centered it on the canvas. His scrunched eyebrows and focused eyes signaled diligence as he gently stroked the outline of a yellow tulip. To him, the drawing of a yellow tulip had a remarkable capacity to either empower or depress himself. Petal by petal, his pursed lips gave way to a satisfied grin. I quickly sighed in relief, embracing the optimism that today would be good day.

My grandfather has Alzheimer's, the long good-bye disease. A self-taught artist, who once captured majestic sceneries of nature, was predicted to lose touch with reality within seven short years. Determined to prolong his neurological functions, I explored the incorporation of his favorite passions into daily therapeutic routines such as solving puzzles, memorizing songs, and drawing flowers. I learned to adjust this curriculum to incorporate his changing concerns, priorities, and values, which has provided ten more years of happiness. Through this relationship, I internalized the power of preventative medicine and the importance of recognizing emotional, mental, and spiritual health concerns in addition to physical ailments. I was immediately hooked to the tenets unique to osteopathic medicine.

Conversations with my grandfather triggered a newfound fascination of the human mind and its intricate connection to the human body. As a medical scribe in the Emergency Department, I relish speculating the mind's mysteries in psychiatric cases. From the hundreds of patient interactions I saw, one truly gravitated me toward the medical profession due to the physician's unique ability to connect with the patient. "Shut the door," the patient hollered. While I was slightly taken aback by the patient's paranoia, I was inspired by the physician's ability to retain a therapeutic nature by demonstrating deference and thoroughly addressing the patient's emotions and concerns. The physician demonstrated compassion and approached the case not as a set of symptoms, but the patient as a whole, which encouraged the patient to regain eye contact and illustrate his horrific visual hallucinations. This experience highlighted how sensitivity, empathy, and compassion underlie human connection, a relationship that must be met before the advancement of any other pursuits. As a medical scribe, I have a responsibility to intently listen and preserve the patient's story in the chart. However, I learned much more than efficient documentation. Just like these physicians, I aspire to become a physician who looks beyond patients' biochemistry and showcases compassion to fully advocate and encourage patients to regain their medical agency. To gain additional direct patient interactions, I began shadowing osteopathic physicians, in which I had a rare opportunity to serve an integral role in the care of a patient. An elderly female Korean patient entered the operating room stricken with worry and fear about her cardiac bypass surgery. She did not speak English and I sensed that her fear originated from uncertainty and a lack of communication. As I am fluent in Korean, I respectfully offered to translate. In just a few words, the patient's eyes widened and displayed signs of relief as she communicated, "I feel safer with you." Once I realized speaking in native tongue instantly created trust, I continued to assuage her fears by intently listening and understanding her story. My time as a medical scribe taught me the importance of relaying compassion and earning trust, but this particular experience was monumental because I had a unique opportunity to develop that trust, feel it, and internalize the power of human connection during her most vulnerable times.

When I see yellow tulips I do not think of the loss and hardships my family endured but of the prevailing cast of hope, perseverance, and fortitude of one's fight for their health. My personal experiences and clinical observations drove my passion for osteopathic medicine, whose holistic principles closely align with my values. Health is the greatest possession an individual owns and becoming an integral part of a patient's emotional narrative in securing their health will give me a sense of reward that no other profession can offer. I am eager to deliver culturally competent and sensitive care by integrating my growing educational principles and skills in concert with my concern for others to play a consequential role in helping them draw their own yellow tulip.

From all the hours spent in writing my personal statement and also discussing how to write an impactful personal statement with my advisers, I put together a list of guidelines of what to do and what not to do while writing a personal statement. I hope this guideline can assist you in writing an impactful personal statement.

Guidelines for Writing a Personal Statement
Adapted from Northwestern HPA "Writing a Personal Statement" (Northwestern University., n.d.)

Make it personal
The personal statement (PS) is an opportunity to express your passion, motivation, values, background, and beliefs. Prior to drafting a PS, ask yourself if there are any experiences, events, or people that helped spark your interest in medicine. Share your own narrative. If you believe that your personal statement can represent another student, then your PS is not fully representing who you are.

Logistics
AMCAS allows 5300 characters and ACCOMAS allows 4500 characters (including spaces). For anyone applying to public Texas schools, they use a separate application system named TMDSAS which allows 5000 characters & 2 optional essays [21].

Why Medicine
The PS must relate why you want to pursue medicine. This may be expressed from any events that occurred during your childhood, while shadowing physicians, or any other experiences that inspired you to pursue medicine. Do not list the experience, but rather, explain what traits, qualities, or reflections you gained from any experiences. Attempt to connect your reflections to your own traits and qualities and explain how those competencies will help you become the physician you want to be.

Personal Experiences
Using any past experiences or events to explain your motivation to medicine is appropriate and encouraged. However, avoid solely using extensive references during your childhood to explain why you want to pursue medicine. You must also convince the admissions committee that you have made a well-informed decision by confirming your desires to pursue medi-

cine. Therefore, use multiple experiences to explain your initial motivation of medicine, how you continued to seek breath, and how you confirmed your desires to pursue medicine. This will demonstrate that you have a full understanding and are making a mature decision to pursue medicine.

Avoid Listing Experiences

Do not merely list experiences in your PS. This is what the Work&Activities section is for. Rather, explain your thoughts and reflections from your experiences. Allow the PS to be an opportunity for you to provide new information that is not available anywhere else in your application.

Positive Tone

This is something I struggled with during my earlier drafts. Do not lecture the admissions officers about what you feel is wrong about "the system." Rather, present your own passion, goals, and hope in a positive tone. You can address what is wrong with 'the system" once you are in it.

Miscellaneous

Avoid cliché statements such as "I want to help others" and "I want to help humanity." It is more effective to demonstrate your sincere interest in helping others by your experiences. Avoid using quotes in your essay unless you feel that it reflects something important about you. Most often, the quotes aren't as unique as you think.

Take Advantage of your Resources

1. The Writing Place: Most undergraduate institution has a writing place that you can get feedback on your writing for free
2. Health Adviser: Develop a good relationship with your premed health adviser. Run your essays through your adviser.
3. Essay Workshop 101: https://www.studentdoctor.net/essays/

Possible Writing Topics for a Personal Statement[21]

Adapted from Northwestern HPA "Writing a Personal Statement" (Northwestern University., n.d.

Motivation for Medicine
- Who or what inspired you?
- How has it evolved with time?
- Is there a specific event that is driving you?
- How do you feel about experiences with death or illness?
- How have you confirmed your desires?

Personal/Family Background
- Unusual obstacles faced
- Hardships that shaped who you are
- Exposure to illness
- Study Abroad or Medical Brigade experiences

Work or Volunteer Experiences
- Work Experience
- Volunteer Experience
- Personal satisfaction or realizations from these experiences
- Time management or leadership qualities gained
- Do not include more than 3-4 experiences in your personal statement. Remember, quality over quantity.

Non-Traditional Applicant
- Will have to highlight the maturity you have gained
- What made you want to switch professions and pursue medicine?
- Deep reflections from your previous work experiences

Personal Philosophy in Religion or Politics
- Can be a risky topic to write about because it is hard to be succinct, and your views may be controversial
- Do not come across as narrow-minded, inflexible, intolerant, or egotistical

- If you choose to write about philosophy, you must relate to your interest in medicine

Personal Statement (& Interview) Brainstorming Questions[21]

Adapted from Northwestern HPA "Writing a Personal Statement" (Northwestern University., n.d.)

Tell me about yourself

- How has your environment shaped who you are and why you want to become a health professional (Example: Do you live in a medically underserved area?)
- How has your family or community members influenced your development
- Are you from a disadvantaged background? If so, describe how these factors shaped you
- How have you grown as a person?
- What are your passion, interests, and hobbies?
- Are you a part of any community including cultural, social, or athletic groups?

How have you prepared to become a health care professional

- Why did you decide to pursue medicine?
- How did you demonstrate your desire for medicine?
- What characteristics or competencies do you think a physician should possess? How do these characteristics relate to your personal characteristics?
- What are your professional goals?
- How have you worked with a diverse group of patients and health care professionals?
- How have you been involved in scientific research?
- If you could not become a medical professional, what other careers or plans have you considered?

Challenges in Life

- What challenges have you faced in life and how did you grow from this experience?
- How can you apply what you learned to the future?

- Has this experience made you more empathic? Humble? Compassionate? Dedicated?
- Before writing about a challenge in your life, think first, would I have become a different person if I did not face this challenge. If you wouldn't have become a different person, then perhaps this isn't as significant as you thought it would be.

Compentencias and Values

- What are you core beliefs or values? How have you come to develop your beliefs or values?
- How have you demonstrated the ability to interact with people from different ethnic, cultural, or religious backgrounds?
- Do you intend to serve an underserved community? How have you demonstrated your commitment to serve this population?
- How have you demonstrated a strong work ethic? Leadership qualities? Time management? Compassion? Commitment to medicine?
- Review the *AAMC Anatomy of an Applicant Self-Assessment Guide* for information about competencies. How are these core competencies (below) reflected in your application?
  Service Orientation, Social Skills, Cultural Competences, Teamwork, Oral communication, Ethical Responsibility, Reliability & Dependability, Resilience & Adaptability, and Capacity for Improvement. You can find the full list of AAMC competencies here: https://students-residents.aamc.org/applying-medical-school/article/core-competencies/

Work&Activities

The Work & Activities (W&A) section of the primary statement is an opportunity for you to list and explain briefly of all your experiences. You can think that the W&A is an extended version of a resume. Since the W&A must be submitted along with the personal statement, I found it beneficial to work on the W&A section whenever I was taking a break from the Personal statement.

The W&A format is similar between the AMCAS and AACOMAS; however, there are a couple of logistical differences. If you are applying to medical school, you may be applying to both DO and MD schools. While the two applications are relatively similar, there are a few differences in character counts/limits for the DO application to keep in mind while you are drafting your essays and activities sections! In this section, I highlight the differences between the two AMCAS and AACOMAS applications:

AMCAS (MD Program) WORK & ACTIVITIES[22]
Adapted from Northwestern HPA "Work and Activities" (Northwestern University., n.d.)

- A maximum of **15** Work & Activities entries are allowed. Since medical schools prefer quantity over quality, admissions will prefer significant experiences that applicants have engaged over a longer period of time. Do not feel pressured that you must list all 15 activities. Again, quality over quantity!
- Since 15 entries are permitted, you are allowed to group experiences if they are under a similar category. For example, if you have multiple shadowing experiences, group all the shadowing experiences together under 1 category. Furthermore, although there is not a hard fast rule about including high school experiences, college experiences are preferred.
- For every experience/activity you have completed, you will be asked to select an experience type. You will have to write the experience name, the duration of the experience, the name of the organization that it was a part of. You will also have to list a reference name/contact information (mentor, adviser, director) who will be able

to vouch that you were a part of that experience in the event the admissions officers decide to give them a call. Lastly, you will have to write a description of the experience. Below you will find all the necessary components that you will fill out on the Work&Activities section.

Work & Activities Entries [22]

Adapted from Northwestern HPA "AMCAS Work and Activities/Common Secondary Prompts" (Northwestern University., n.d.)

1. ### Select Experience Type from the following categories

Artistic Endeavors	Volunteer - Medical Community Service	Volunteer – Non-Medical Community Service
Conference Attended	Extracurricular Activities	Hobbies
Honors/Awards/ Recognition	Intercollegiate Athletics	Leadership – Not Listed Elsewhere
Military Services	Paid Employment – Medical	Paid Employment – Non-Medical
Presentations/Posters	Publications	Research/Lab
Teaching/Tutoring/ Teaching Assistant	Physician Shadowing/ Clinical Observation	Other

2. ### Experience Name: 60 character limit
3. ### Start Date/End Date/Total # of Hours/Repeated?
   You may add up to 4 time periods by choosing "repeated." This is helpful for seasonal only experiences. Example: hospital volunteer every summer
4. ### Organization Name/Country/City
5. ### Contact's Name/Title/Phone or Email
   Unlike AACOMAS, it is mandatory that you list the contact information. You must enter either a contact's phone or Email address
6. ### Experience Description
   700 Character Limit (including spaces). Use this space to speak about your leadership position, activity, value, and significance of activity.

7. **Most Meaningful Experience (MME)**

You may select up to 3 experiences in which you think is your most meaningful experience. If you check the box, an additional text box of 1325 characters (including spaces) will appear.

Here is the MME prompt: *This is your opportunity to summarize why you have selected this experience as one of your most meaningful. In your remarks, you might consider the transformative nature of the experience, the impact you made while engaging in the experience, and the personal growth you experienced as a result of your participation.*

Nahee Park Work & Activities Sample Essay

Most Meaningful: Yes
Experience Type: Research/Lab
Experience Name: Independent Student Researcher
Organization Name: XXX
Date: Sept 2015-Dec 2017
Hours: 1467
Contact Information: XXX

Experience Description:
I joined the XXX research team to investigate how socioeconomic status affects Asthma or Cardiovascular diseases in adolescents. Lab experiences included culturing and analyzing blood samples, data entry, and gathering post-clinic surveys.

Dr. XXX's Lab investigates molecular genetics of circadian rhythm (CR) using mouse and fly genetics. I carried out two independent projects under the assistance of my mentor XXX: investigating the role of non-specific cationic channel (NALCN) in Mammalian CR and if manipulating synapse formation in *Drosophila* brain alters sleep drive. I was awarded three highly competitive research grants for all three projects.

Most Meaningful Essay (MME)
Research nourished my intellectual curiosity as I mastered technical skills, analyzed the gap in sleep research, and fostered my problem-solving abilities by initiating, organizing, and developing my independent project. I took ownership of a complex project by generating transgenic flies, quantifying sleep behavior, and analyzing results. By my senior year, I trained new undergraduate students on fly genetics. Performing research gave me a sense of reward and excitement for tackling a gap in the field that has never been researched before.

This research experience was crucial in my scholarly growth, as it demanded analytical abilities, assertiveness, resilience, and intellectual creativity to identify scientific problems, modify structural changes, and adapt procedures. Furthermore, since research is a collaborative art, I had the opportunity to expand my interpersonal skills and effectively communicate my ideas to lab members during lab presentations. My experiences of being an effective team player and providing constructive criticism will be essential in any hospital setting to achieve a common goal. I hope to apply my comprehensive set of skills acquired as a researcher to become a detail-oriented, passionate, and enthusiastic medical student and physician.

Nahee Park Work & Activities Sample Essay

Most Meaningful: No
Experience Type: Physician Shadowing/ Clinical Observation
Experience Name: Shadowing Various Physicians
Organization Name: Unity Point Methodist Hospital/ OSF Hospital/ Northwestern Hospital
Date: July 2014 – March 2018
Hours: 82
Contact Information: XXX
Experience Description:
A breakdown of clinical observations below:
Pediatrics, Cardiology, Radiology, Endocrinology, General Surgery, ICU, NICU, Infectious Diseases, OBGYN, Hematology
In shadowing physicians, I learned that medicine is not just about physicians treating a set of symptoms, but recognizing their direct significance to patients and their families. I also recognized personal sacrifices physicians make every day such as getting 4 hours of sleep and missing their son's basketball game. Despite the expansive paperwork, I admired the collaborative atmosphere where everyone in the hospital had the same goal: having the best interest for the patient.

Nahee Park Work & Activities Sample Essay

Most Meaningful: No
Experience Type: Community Service Volunteer - Medical
Experience Name: Emergency Department, Pre/Post Op Volunteer, Medical Clinic Volunteer
Organization Name: Unity Point Methodist Hospital/ Presence St. Francis Hospital/United Methodist Church Loaves and Fish (MCL&F)
Date: Dec 2015 – February 2018
Hours: 120

Contact Information: XXX

Experience Description:

I have been involved in two clinical volunteer programs. My duties as a hospital volunteer included directing patients to rooms, restocking, and turning over exam rooms. I enjoyed the relationships developed with the patients and healthcare team members. Determined to create a welcoming environment, I strove to comfort frightened children by reading books and offered distressed families drinks and snacks to ease their wait. As a MCL&F clinic volunteer, I measured blood pressure and lead preventative care education to those in need. A simple "Oh, yes I needed my blood pressure to be taken" gave me a sense of fulfillment for playing an integral role in the care of my community members.

Nahee Park Work & Activities Sample Essay

Most Meaningful: No

Experience Type: Honors/Awards/Recognition

Experience Name: Korean Scholarship Recipient of Academic and Service Honor

Organization Name: Korean-American Scientists and Engineers Association (KSEA)/ Korean Honor Scholarship (KHS)

Date: 5/15/2017

Hours: n/a

Contact Information: XXX

Experience Description:

Awarded the prestigious KSEA Scholarship of $1000, which recognizes 20 students of Korean heritage in the United States who demonstrate stellar academic performance, leadership, and community service. I was also awarded the KHS of $1000, which selects two outstanding students of Korean heritage in Midwest states with high academic achievement, dedication to service, and high leadership qualities for future professional careers. Both scholarships reflect my intellectual achievements, passion for service, and strong leadership skills in instilling a positive social change in my community.

Nahee Park Work & Activities Sample Essay

Most Meaningful: No

Experience Type: Paid Employment - Medical

Experience Name: Emergency Department Medical Scribe

Organization Name: ScribeAmerica

Date: Feb 5 2017 – April 9 2019

Hours: 1400

Nahee Park

Contact Information: XXX

Experience Description:

Being a Medical Scribe offers personal collaboration with physicians by performing documentation, gathering patient's charts, and delivering efficient patient care. As a scribe, I have come to appreciate the importance of creative communication skills, compassion, and empathy in delivering the best patient care possible. Through this experience, I have gained a deep understanding of medical terminology and also learned how to anticipate what a professional healthcare provider needs. My experiences in efficiently documenting charts along with small habits obtained from successful physicians will provide a great stepping-stone in my career of medicine.

Nahee Park Work & Activities Sample Essay

Most Meaningful: No

Experience Type: Paid Employment - Nonmedical

Experience Name: Biology and Chemistry SAT Subject and AP Tutor

Organization Name: LanguageWill

Date: 3/17/2018 – May 1 2019

Hours: 350

Contact Information: XXX

Experience Description:

LanguageWill is tutoring company in South Korea that offers SAT and AP tutoring services to Korean students who are preparing to attend college in the United States. Through an online virtual system, I tutor Biology and Chemistry SAT and AP tests to students in Korean. This was my first virtual mentorship speaking in a language associated to a country I have never lived in. I was exposed to countless physical, cultural, and language barriers. However, through preparation, confidence, creativity, and utilizing the tools that I had developed in previous tutor experiences, I am able to clearly communicate the concepts and strategically cater curriculum that fit their individual needs.

Nahee Park Work & Activities Sample Essay

Most Meaningful: No

Experience Type: Hobbies

Experience Name: Origami, Lego building, friendship bracelet, embroidery

Organization Name: N/A

Date: June 2001 – Aug 1 2019

Hours: N/A

Experience Description:

As a child, I have always been fascinated in building significant objects from scratch. Whether it's shaping 3D masterpieces from paper, constructing a monument with 4x2 lego bricks, or stitching beautiful designs from thread, I find the process relaxing, fulfilling, and exciting. These activities have helped me to develop dexterity, creativity, mental acuity, and patience. I have shared my knowledge and talent of making origami creations to children with autism at Haley's Playground, senior citizens at retirement homes, and children at church. It gives me great fulfillment when my childhood hobby inspires others to enjoy and make these hobbies their own.

AACOMAS WORK & ACTIVITIES

Unlike the AMCAS where you can list up to 15 entries that includes experiences and awards, the AACOMAS differentiates between experiences and achievements. Also, there is an unlimited number of entries you can list; however, medical schools prefer quality of quantity. Therefore only include entries that you think are significant. While high school experiences can be submitted, college experiences are preferred. After submission, you can add more experiences and achievements; however, you cannot make previous changes.

Experiences Entries[23]

1. Select Experience Type from 4 categories

Non-Healthcare Employment, Extracurricular Activities, Non-Healthcare Volunteer or Community Service, and Health Care Experience

2. Organization

Name, Country, State

3. Supervisor (Optional but recommended)

Name, Title, Phone or Email

4. Experience Date

Start & End Date, Check if continuing experience, Status (Full-Time, Part-Time, Temporary)

5. Experience Details

Title, Type of Recognition (Compensated, Academic Credit, Volunteer), Total Hours (Average Weekly Hours, Number of Weeks)

6. Experience Description

600 Character Limit (including spaces) to describe your experience, leadership role, & what you have learned

Achievement Entries[24]

1. Select Achievement Type from 5 categories
Award, Honors, Presentation, Publications, or Scholarships
2. Name of Achievement
3. Name of Presenting Organization (Optional)
4. Issued Date (optional)
5. Achievement Description
600 character limit (including spaces) to describe achievement

Secondary Application

First of all, congratulations on submitting your primary applications! You have come a long way and you should be proud of your efforts thus far. If you were like me, you probably submitted your primary application by June 1st, and now you are wondering what to do until July when the secondary applications will start to roll in your email inbox. Fear not – I will give you something to keep you busy during June.

If you applied to 30-40 medical schools, the secondary application will be an haunting process. Since most medical schools have approximately 3-5 secondary questions per secondary application, this means you are looking to submit over 100 essays in total. Since some schools have a strict deadline of 2 weeks to submit the secondary application, it will be a huge advantage to pre-write your secondary essays during the month of June. Ideally, you will be done writing secondary essays around July. This will allow you to immediately submit your secondary applications as soon as you receive the secondary application invitation. Because I was pre-writing my secondary essays, I was able to finalize and submit my secondary application about 3-4 days after I received it.

I am thinking you have two questions for me right now:

1. **How do I know which medical schools will offer me to write a secondary application? I do not want to waste my time writing a secondary application to a school if I'm not going to get a secondary application invitation.** This is a great question and something that was on my mind before pre-writing my secondary essays. This is another reason why you should subscribe to MSAR (Medical School Admission Requirement) for $28 through the official AAMC website. The MSAR website will indicate if they screen students for secondaries. I believe that about 70% of the medical schools automatically send a secondary application to all students. About 20% medical schools will send secondaries to applicants that pass a minimum MCAT score (usually 499, 500). There are only a few medical schools that will do a heavy holistic screen of your application before sending a secondary. From my personal experience, I did not get a secondary from UCLA and University of Washington. University of Colorado is another school that does a moderate screen and will send secondaries to 50-60% of those that submit a primary statement. Also, a few schools such as Indiana University Medical School do not have secondary essays. Therefore, check out MSAR to see what medical schools are more likely to send out secondaries.

2. **How can do I know the secondary writing prompts from medical schools before getting a secondary application invitation?**

Luckily, there are numerous resources online where you can search for "medical school secondary application prompts" before you receive the invitation. Albeit, these prompts would be last year's prompts. The good news is that medical schools often re-use their prompts. Personally, I only had 3-4 prompts that differed from their previous year's prompts. Therefore, I strongly encourage you to search up the previous year's secondary prompts and begin to write them.

♠ Personally, I used this website to search medical school secondary prompts[25]:
http://www.passportadmissions.com/students/medical-schools-by-state/
This is a free resource open to the public.

Many schools will have similar secondary questions which means that you can definitely recycle your essays if appropriate. Of course, you will still have to somewhat tailor the essays for each medical school (especially for school specific questions), however, there are a reoccurring theme of essays including Diversity, Personal Challenge, Research, & Gap Year questions. Prior to writing your secondary essays, I encourage you to brainstorm ideas within each theme and write a rough draft. Since the word limit differs for every school, try to stay at about 2000-3000 characters for each essay. This will allow you to be flexible in tailoring your essay to each school. I have grouped similar questions from different medical schools. I also included how I addressed each themed question at the end of this section.

The medical school secondary questions below were taken from http://www.passportadmissions.com/students/medical-schools-by-state/
Passport Admissions. Medical School Secondary Prompts. (n.d.),

Personal Challenge Questions[25]

This essay will be an opportunity for you to show resilience, self-insight, and personal growth. Here are some examples from medical schools:

[Loyola Medical School] Loyola seeks students who are resourceful and lifelong learners who are both self-aware and adaptable. Please describe a personal or professional challenge or conflict that you have experienced. How did you resolve it? What skills, resources and/or strategies did you employ? DO NOT write about the MCAT, a course, or an academic issue. (500 words max)

[RUSH] Describe a challenging situation in which you did not agree with a directive/rule and how you handled this. (1000 characters)

[UIC] Describe a stressful situation that you have experienced. Please detail your reaction, how you managed the situation, and what you learned that will help you handle a similar circumstance in the future

[Rosalind Franklin] In the space provided, please discuss challenges in your journey to applying to medical school. (100 words)

[MCW – Medical College of Wisconsin] Describe a time when you found a creative solution to a challenging or unfamiliar situation. Include what you learned from the experience. (2000 characters)

[Wake Forest] What obstacles or challenges have you experienced and how have you dealt with them (400 words or less)

[UNC Chapel Hill] We have all tried something and failed, whether it was something big or something small. Describe a situation or an experience you had when you realized that you were not up to the task, and tell us what life-lessons you learned from this experience

[DUKE] Describe a situation where you failed. What did you learn from the experience? Describe at least one functional impact of the experience. (600 words)

[Case Western] The admissions committee is interested in gaining more insight into you as a person. Please describe a significant personal challenge you have faced, one which you feel has helped to shape you as a person. Examples may include a moral or ethical dilemma, a situation of personal adversity, or a hurdle in your life that you worked hard to overcome. Please include how you got through the experience and what you learned about yourself as a result. Please

limit your response to 1 page (about 3,500 characters), and leave a blank line between paragraphs

*[**West Virginia**] Describe a situation where you had to overcome adversity; include lessons learned and how you think it will affect your career as a future physician*

*[**Iowa**] Describe any unique personal characteristics and obstacles you may have overcome that will contribute to the diversity of, and bring educational benefits to, the entering class*

(Medical School Secondary Prompts, n.d.)

Nahee Park Sample Essay to the Challenge Question

Four months ago, I had the honor of becoming a part-time tutor for a tutoring company located in South Korea. As this tutoring company gears toward preparing South Korean students to study at a college in the United States, my responsibilities included tutoring on various standardized tests to native Korean students through virtual video systems. Believing that I was armed with the necessary knowledge, resources, and experiences, I was confident that I could guide my high school students to success.

Since the students only had a couple of months before their AP or SAT Subject exams, I created a comprehensive schedule that included homework assignments, reading assignments, and practice tests. Each tutoring session began with a quick review of previous concepts. When students no longer had questions, I moved on to the next chapters and ended each session with students solving practice problems. As students began to demonstrate drastic improvements in their scores, I believed that my curriculum and strategic approach was a success. For the next two months, I was extremely proud of my students for their accomplishment and dedication in learning.

However, shortly after, I was surprised when half of my students suddenly dropped out of tutoring. I was immediately devastated and began to reflect on what I had done wrong. I looked through my weekly summary reports to analyze if the students' score improvements were not enough or if my Korean language was not fluent enough. When I called the director to understand what I could do to improve, I was instantly humbled by his statement. He stated that since I was completely enamored with my approach, I had forgotten to incorporate their feedback and cater to their needs. After receiving this constructive criticism, I was shocked by the truth of his words. I recognized that I was so captivated by my own curriculum that I never asked if my students were satisfied or if there was anything I could do to improve the learning experience.

Through this humbling experience, I learned that in any service position, it is less about my own thought processes and myself. While being confident and grounded in our values and motives, we must demonstrate humility and acknowledge the concerns and feedback of others. This humbling experience prompts me to evaluate my motives and constantly receive feedback on my performance. I am grateful for what I have learned as these characteristics will be important when interacting with peers and patients. When discussing a medical intervention with a patient or sharing a case with a peer, I believe it is important to work as a team, regularly ask for their opinions, and ensure that all their questions and concerns are thoroughly investigated. Through my learned experiences of tutoring others, I am prepared to keep the patients in mind and ensure that I am exceeding their needs.

♠ What are your thoughts on this essay? I would say that I am not exactly the greatest fan of this personal challenge/failure essay. Luckily, I realized it after I submitted it to only 1 school. The reason why I shared this essay is because I think it will be noteworthy to discuss what went wrong here:

I recall my adviser telling me to write about a "life challenging event" that helped me grow as a person. She asked me the question, "If you never experienced this particular challenge, would it have changed who you are as a person?" My answer to my essay above was a straight up NO. I probably would have been the same person whether or not I experienced this particular challenge. Perhaps this is why this particular challenging story does not create a huge impact.

On the other hand, I believe that not all challenging stories have to be dramatic. Granted, I am sure that dramatic stories will be easier to write; however, don't stretch it especially if you do not have one. Play with what you have. I am sure you have learned at least something with every event, no matter how small the event.

Diversity Questions[25]

This essay will be an opportunity for you to share your unique traits, characteristics, or circumstances. This can include culture, race, ethnicity, sexual orientation, gender identity, life experiences, work experiences, perspectives, socioeconomic status, environment, etc. Although race and ethnicity certainly contribute to diversity, there are many other factors that can contribute to your diversity. Here are some examples from medical schools:

[Loyola] How will you contribute to the diversity of the Stritch student body and community? Specifically, what unique traits, identities, experiences, skills and perspectives will you contribute?

[RUSH] Describe personal attributes you possess or life experiences you have had that will enable you to better understand patients with a culture different from your own. Please include your self-reflection on how this experience has changed your insights, beliefs, and/or values. (1000 characters)

[Northwestern-Feinberg] Everyone has their own narrative. Please provide more detail about your cultural background and how you would enrich the Northwestern community. (200 words)

[Rosalind Franklin] In the space provided, please include a statement that specifically address how, if admitted to our program, your admission would contribute to the diversity of the Chicago Medical School at Rosalind Franklin University of Medicine and Science community

[University of Michigan] At the University of Michigan Medical School, we are committed to building a superb educational community with students of diverse talents, experiences, opinions, and backgrounds. What would you as an individual bring to our medical school community? Do not exceed 1500 characters (about 250 words).

[Western Michigan] Describe what you bring to the practice of medicine - your values, skills, talents, and life experiences - and how you add to the cultural, ethnic, and socioeconomic diversity of the medical profession.

[Mayo] Please tell us how you would contribute to the diversity of your medical school class at Mayo

[DUKE] Tell us more about who you are. You may provide additional information that expands your self-identity where gender identification, racial and/or ethnic self description, geographic origin, socioeconomic, academic, and/or other characteristics that define who you are as you contemplate a career that will interface with

people who are similar AND dissimilar to you. You will have the opportunity below to tell us how you wish to be addressed, recognized and treated (500 words)

[U Michigan] At the University of Michigan Medical School, we are committed to building a superb educational community with students of diverse talents, experiences, opinions, and backgrounds. What would you as an individual bring to our medical school community? Do not exceed 1500 characters (about 250 words/some say 1500cc)

[Wake Forest] The Committee on Admissions values diversity as an important factor in the educational mission of the Wake Forest School of Medicine. How will you contribute to the diversity of your medical school class and to the medical community in general? (400 words or less).

[Virginia Tech Carilion] Each member of the VTC community has a unique and enriching life-story. Interactions with heterogeneous populations increase compassion, understanding, and the ability to communicate effectively and respectfully with others. Explain how your life experience has shaped your world view, describe your approach to people who see the world differently, and relate how you would enrich the VTC community

(Medical School Secondary Prompts, n.d.)

Nahee Park Sample Essay to the Diversity Question

My passion for academic reform stems from the challenges I faced as a second generation Korean-American in a predominantly Caucasian school. As a student, the stereotypes that Asians were quiet and smart constantly lurked over me as my greatest fear was failing to exceed the expectations attached to my ethnic and cultural background. Nevertheless, I recognized the fruitful aspects of the expectations as it challenged me to embrace hard work, perseverance, and resilience. When I saw how my cultural background positively contributed to my school performance, I was driven to promote academic reform in underserved communities. In high school, I recalled the wide disparities in educational expenditures in the state of Illinois and offered solutions to close the disparities in education to the state senators. Although my ideas were ultimately dismissed, I recognized the power and inspiration my voice had brought to my community. When I arrived to my college campus, a particular high school intrigued me. The school itself was ranked to be in one of the wealthiest school districts; however, over 40% of the students were below the poverty line. Therefore, I developed the Illuminate Mentorship Program to provide standardized tests and college-prep guidance to underserved students. My commitment in social justice allowed me to perceive inequality in our communities, fight for the justice of our community members, and instill solutions to improve the lives of individuals that are dissimilar to me.

Nevertheless, my ethnic and cultural backgrounds have allowed me to improve the lives of individuals who share my culture. For instance, I had an opportunity to translate for an elderly Korean woman who refused to receive a blood transfusion. Attributing the patient's fear to a language barrier, I was driven to facilitate the patient in obtaining adequate healthcare. After a lengthy discussion in Korean, it was apparent that the patient depended on oriental medicine and was unfamiliar with the practices of Western medicine. Fortunately, my yearly trips to South Korea and my understanding of oriental medicine philosophies from my grandmother, a retired Korean Oriental Pharmacist, enabled me to internalize the patient's concerns and relay her cultural ideologies to the physician. Under careful guidance of the physician, I used my native fluency in Korean with my limited, yet familiar knowledge in oriental medicine to gain her trust and articulate the idea of receiving a blood transfusion along with her daily herbal regimen. This experience prompts me to embrace my unique culture and expertise, apply these elements to patient-advocacy, and bring greater perspectives to classroom discussions.

Overall, I believe that my self-identity as a second generation Korean-American has influenced my desire not only to immerse in communities of different religious and ethnic backgrounds, but also to personally connect with individuals who share my language and cultural ideologies. Through my diverse encounters and cultural awareness, I am eager to bring a comprehensive view and further XXX School of Medicine's devotion of transforming medicine and advocating for the wellbeing of patients.

Gap Year Experience[25]

This essay will be an opportunity for you to share what you have done, or will be doing for your gap year. If you are not taking a gap year, then you will skip this question. Here are some examples from medical schools:

[Oakland] If you have already graduated, briefly summarize your activities since graduation (400 words)

[Wake Forest] If you have already received your bachelor's degree, please describe what you have been doing since graduation and your plans for the upcoming year (200 words or less)

[Tulane University] What have you been pursuing since gradu-

ation? (150 words)

[Emory] List your entire curriculum plan for the current academic year. If you are not currently in school, please briefly describe your plans for the coming year (200 words)

[Northwestern-Feinberg] If you have (or expect to have) a year or more between college graduation and medical school matriculation, describe your activities and/or plan. (200 words)

[Iowa] If you are not currently in a degree-seeking program, please indicate what you will be doing from the time you complete this secondary application to the start of medical school (1500 cc)

(Medical School Secondary Prompts, n.d.)

Nahee Park Sample Essay to the Gap Year Question

In order to gain more exposure and a practical context of the patient-physician interaction, I became a full-time emergency department medical scribe. By partnering with a physician, I expedite the process of a patient's visit by documenting their history of illness, lab results, and diagnosis. As a result, my responsibilities increase direct physician-patient interaction and allow physicians to attend to more patients. As a scribe, I enjoy observing the interaction, anticipating diagnosis, and discussing each case personally with physicians to expand my medical knowledge.

Along with working as a full time medical scribe, I am also committed to continuing my passion of tutoring others. I am a part-time SAT subject and AP tutor to Korean students who plan to attend college in the United States. In addition, I am a volunteer at the Peoria Rescue Ministries, which is a non-profit organization that offers recovery programs to victims of abuse, addiction, and homelessness. As a computer educator, I create curriculum and assist residents with basic computer skills such as Microsoft Word and Excel. I am rewarded and inspired to offer women the tools needed for their fresh start toward a positive redirection in life.

Research[25]

If you are applying to a MD/PHD program, then you will definitely will have to articulate about your previous research experiences. Otherwise, if you are a MD applicant, then the research question will be optional.

[DUKE] Critical thinking involves many aspects including curiosity,

comprehension, application and analysis. Describe a time when you have utilized critical thinking. How do you anticipate critical thinking being used as part of your career? (400 words) **This does not have to be research

[U Michigan] If you would like to comment in depth regarding your research background you may answer this optional question. How would your past experiences in laboratory-based research on fundamental problems in the biological and biomedical sciences motivate you to pursue similar efforts as a physician-scientist? Do not exceed 1500 characters.

[Case Western] One of the four pillars of the Western Reserve2 Curriculum is Research and Scholarship. Although research is not a pre-requisite requirement for the University Program, if you have participated in research or another scholarly project please tell us about it. Describe your experience, including the question you pursued and how you approached it, your results and interpretation of the results, and most importantly, any thoughts about what this experience meant to you

(Medical School Secondary Prompts, n.d.)

Nahee Park Sample Essay to the Research Question [Case Western]

I have always wondered why and how we sleep. Surprisingly, while sleep is an important process that is conserved in every animal species, the regulation of sleep is poorly understood. Previous research studies identified ten neuromodulators in the Drosophila, which alter sleep rebound after sleep deprivation. However, it is unclear where these neuromodulators act on sleep homeostasis in the fly brain. To understand how brain function is impaired after sleep loss, I investigated where known modulators of sleep homeostasis regulate sleep after sleep deprivation in *Drosophila* flies.

To identify where neuromodulators act, three genes were selected where a knockout construct (null mutant), UAS rescue construct, and RNAi for the gene of interest are available. The selected genes are *creb2, Ecdysone receptor,* and *dFmr1,* the Drosophila homolog of the human Fragile X mental retardation gene. As the neuromodulator *dFrm1* has been shown to have high expression levels in the mushroom body region, a region that is predicted to regulate sleep and intellectual ability, I hypothesized that the main location of restoring impaired sleep would be found in the mushroom bodies of the brain. To carry out this project, sleep behavior was measured by placing flies in the Drosophila activity monitoring system. Flies were then placed in a rotating mechanical device to deprive sleep. Rebound sleep was quantified as an increase in sleep compared to the baseline.

The sleep behaviors of flies were recorded and analyzed with statistical computations. As expected, entirely knocking out *dFrm1* displayed impaired rebound sleep. However, knocking out specific components of *dFrm1* via RNAi technique produced varying sleep rebound behavior. The most promising RNAi line displayed high rebound sleep as it recovered approximately 50% of sleep loss in 24 hours. Therefore, restoring the gene function of *d-Frm1* enhanced rebound sleep after sleep deprivation. This result supports that *dFrm1* is important for sleep regulation. As this gene is heavily expressed in the mushroom body, the results support my hypothesis that the restoration of impaired sleep may occur in the mushroom bodies. Unfortunately, all the other lines were statistically insignificant.

Conducting research provided me with the opportunity to gain incredible insight, knowledge, and breath in the world of research. This independent project enhanced my critical thinking skills as it required that I identify a gap in the field, comprehend the problem, apply concepts, and analyze results. I believe that the aspects of critical thinking and problem-solving skills are important in the field of medicine. For example, a physician must identify which procedures, blood work, or imaging to perform based on a patient's narrative and symptoms. From the results of each intervention, physicians can begin to use a process of elimination to form a diagnosis. Overall, each step of the medical intervention requires aspects of critical thinking to identify a treatment plan and ultimately enhance the wellbeing of a patient. I enjoyed performing research due to the problem-solving aspects in each step of the research journey. Similarly, I am excited to pursue a career as a physician, apply critical thinking skills, and enhance lifelong learning.

Why XXX Medical School

This school specific question will appear in most secondary essays. It will appear the following formats:

- Why are you applying to our medical school?
- Please discuss your interest in XXX Medical School and how you can contribute to our school's mission
- Please explain your reasons for applying to XXX Medical School.

♠ Prior to answering this essay question, you will have to spend time researching the school's website to learn more about a particular medical school. Make sure to know the school's mission and understand how well your values, beliefs, or commitment align with their mission. Does the school have any programs, pathways, or opportunities that are unique to the school? The core of the "Why School" essay will be similar because it should represent your interests and passion (which, I hope, should be consistent). However, it is important to tailor it to different schools. If your essay could represent another school, it is not specific enough. Below is an example of how I presented my passion and interests to two different schools.

Why have you chosen to apply to Georgetown University School of Medicine, and how do you think your education at Georgetown will prepare you to become a physician for the future?

(1 page)

Nahee Park: Why Georgetown Essay

My experiences in serving the underserved communities inspired me to become a physician-advocate that perceives healthcare disparities and advocates for the accessibility of healthcare to underserved populations. Tangentially, I also aspire to be a physician-scientist that conducts translational research in neurology to directly improve the health of patients from a scientific perspective. Thus, I am drawn to Georgetown University's MD program due to its Jesuit values of serving others and comprehensive education that combines service opportunities, patient-centered curriculum, and research projects.

The core Jesuit values of GUCM resonates with my personal values of serving others. I believe that becoming a person for others is a core value that stems from the Jesuit education of promoting justice through compassion, service, and faith in God. Although my passion of serving others was shaped by a genuine desire to achieve the greater good, these small acts transitioned into a service that became effortless, and my inner motivations of empathy and compassion enabled the growth of an interconnection with others. Thus, I am especially drawn to GUCM's devotion of service and social justice. At GUCM, I am eager to join the Community of Hope and Hoya Health Academy to support underserved adolescents with academic support, health literacy, and personal guidance. In addition, I wish to immerse myself in the HOYA clinic and the Georgetown Street Medicine Outreach Program to deliver medical attention and essential resources to those facing homelessness or economic hardships. Altogether, pursuing GUCM's meaningful service-learning opportunities will not only allow me to interact with members from diverse cultural and religious backgrounds, but it will prepare me as a culturally sensitive physician who embraces the Jesuit values of solidarity and social responsibility.

In addition, I am drawn to GUCM's comprehensive curriculum that focuses on a collaborative patient-based learning. GUCM's new curriculum of applying clinical experiences with scientific content, simulation practices, and small group discussions allows the formation of contextual knowledge. As I experience greater understanding and retention from learning concepts, re-visiting concepts, and understanding its relationships to a broader context, I believe that this medical curriculum of triadic learning is the perfect academic environment for me. Furthermore, I am interested in the interdisciplinary ideals of the Learning Societies that introduces supportive relationships and co-operative learning. Similarly, my undergraduate institution organized a "peer advisor group" that provided invaluable personalized mentorship, leadership development, and cultural awareness. I believe that GUCM's collaborative and holistic learning community will cultivate my critical interactive skills and provide life-long learning that is imperative as a considerate and skilled physician.

Lastly, GUCM's leading neurology research programs on neurological disorders stimulate my intellectual curiosity. After witnessing the effects of the Alzheimer's disease on my grandfather, I was driven to learn about this disease as an undergraduate researcher. Performing research in neurobiology was exhilarating because I could apply concepts learned during my undergraduate career, master technical skills, and work towards solving a research question of personal relevance. I believe physicians have a responsibility of not only promoting patient care and education, but also applying their medical expertise to foster medical discoveries in advancing the care of patients. Therefore, I am compelled to join The Memory Disorder Program in the Department of Neurology to foster my personal discovery of the Alzheimer's disease and advance the human condition as an innovative physician-scientist.

Overall, GUCM's devotion of patient care and social justice shows their commitment in producing culturally sensitive and compassionate physicians who values the wellbeing of their community members. I believe that GUCM's diverse medical education will give me a comprehensive set of tools to become a culturally competent and impactful physician-advocate and physician-scientist.

What is your specific interest in the MD Program at GW? What opportunities would you take advantage of as a student here? Why? (2000 characters)

Nahee Park: Why George Washington Essay

I am drawn to GW's MD Program due to its comprehensive curriculum that combines integrative learning, service learning projects, and global immersion opportunities. GW's academic curriculum of integrated public health education and urban community health initiatives supplements my values of serving the underserved urban communities. Thus, I am excited to immerse myself in the Community and Urban Health Track and Clinical Public Health Curriculum to fully understand urban health issues and health care systems.

In addition, GW has a unique commitment of service that is demonstrated by its extensive service-learning opportunities. I am thrilled to continue my love of education and service by participating in the Healthy Teen Scholars Learning Community in ISCOPES to discuss adolescent health, provide culturally competent care, and develop health initiative projects which address a community-identified need. Furthermore, partaking in one of GW's Healing Clinics and immersing myself in an outreach program will allow me to deliver accessible healthcare to GW's underserved community members with compassion and sensitivity.

Lastly, I am impressed with GW's global immersion opportunities. As an undergraduate, volunteering in a medical missions trip in Peru gave me a tremendous service-learning perspective. Thus, I hope to pursue global health initiatives by joining the GW Students for Haiti Student Organization. Additionally, I am fascinated with the opportunity to experience an international clinical rotation at the Seoul National University in South Korea. This distinctive program will not only cultivate and diversify my medical education in another country, but it will also give me personal value to study at the Seoul National University, an institution that has educated over three generations of my family. Overall, I believe GW's medical education will equip me with educational principles, resources, and skills to become a culturally sensitive physician-advocate.

Additional Information

This question will be often found at the end of the secondary application and will give you an opportunity to state something that you want to share to the admissions officers. Please be sure not to re-state or highlight anything that you have already written in your primary or secondary essays. This essay is optional, but I encourage you to take advantage of this extra space. Here are some examples:

[Case Western] Is there any further information that you wish to share with the Admissions Committee?

[Loyola] Please use the space below to further explain anything in your application that may help us in our review of your candidacy-gaps or delays in education, academic missteps, or personal chal-

lenges not listed elsewhere, etc (1500 characters)

[Oakland] Is there anything you want the admissions committee to know about your qualifications for medical school that is not already represented in your application materials? Note: This space is provided for new information only, not to promote qualifications already highlighted in your other materials

[Keck Southern California] Is there anything else you would like us to know? If yes, please answer the question in 200 words or less

[Drexel] What else do you feel is important for us to know about you? Please use this space to highlight something not addressed in your application (200 words)

[Thomas Jefferson] Sidney Kimmel does not have required questions, only a prompt asking if you have "any additional information that you would like to share (4,000cc)

(Medical School Secondary Prompts, n.d.)

After drafting these themed based answers, begin writing essays specific to each schools based on their previous year's prompts. If you are applying to 30-40 medical schools, this means that you will be writing approximately 1 medical school secondary application per day in order to be finished by the first week of July.

In my experience, I finished all my essays by July. Before submission, I shared my essays with my brother and sister who were kind enough to proofread my essays. Therefore, when I started receiving secondary invitations on June 29th, I was able to immediately submit my secondary application in the next couple of days. When you begin receiving your secondaries, it is important to know how to organize everything so secondaries do not get lost in your emails. Also be sure to check your spam mail. I believe I received about 2-3 secondary invitations to my spam folder. Here is a template of how you should organize the secondaries you receive.

School Name	Date Received	Date Submitted	Cost $	Username	Password	Application Link

Furthermore, you will soon be receiving an overwhelming amount of emails from medical schools as this is your main method of communication. Imagine this: if you are applying to 30-40 schools and each school sends you 10 emails throughout the span of the application process, that is easily 300-400 emails in your inbox! Therefore, you will have to strategize how to organize your emails. I created folders of medical schools in alphabetical order. I would then move each email to its specific folder.

CHAPTER 13: RECOMMENDATION LETTER

Students should begin brainstorming who they will ask for their letter of recommendations (LOR) in February prior to the medical school application cycle. LOR are important because they allow admission committees to understand an applicant's characteristics such as maturity, work ethic, academic performance, communication skills, teamwork, interpersonal skills, service orientation, organizational skills, character, talents, or other strengths not reflected in the application. Since recommenders have the ability to develop an applicant's overall impression, it is important to choose your recommenders wisely. Remember, admissions officers are dealing with 5,000-1,5000 applications who look similar on paper. Therefore, this is a chance for the admissions to assess if the applicant has determination, commitment, and integrity.

The LOR requirements vary between medical schools. For example, some medical schools are lenient and ask for at least 1 science professor LOR. Other medical schools may have stricter requirements such as having 2 science professors, 1 humanities professor, and 1 volunteer adviser. Therefore, in order to fulfill the LOR requirement for all medicals schools, the most ideal compilation is to get a letter from 2 science professors, 1 research mentor, 1 humanities professor, 1 activities advisor, and 1 MD or DO physician. It is noted that only osteopathic schools recommend or require a DO/MD letter of recommendation. The activities adviser can be anyone from club/organization advisors, research PI/mentor, or volunteer coordinators. Consider asking individuals who know you personally and can assess your abilities, talents, strengths, and characteristics.

♠ I did not have a "non-science" professor letter of recommendation which meant that I couldn't apply to medical schools that required a non-science letter. This restricted me from applying to about 3-4 schools that I was interested in including New York Medical College.

Funny story. I had originally asked for a letter from one of my humanities professor. Although she agreed to write a letter for me in the beginning, I could not get in contact with her after her initial email reply. For the next 5 months I left numerous emails, phone calls, and office visits; however, she was unreachable. To this day, I do not know what happened to her.

In order to be able to select recommenders that know you the best, it is pertinent that you develop a relationship with them. Therefore, start meeting with your recommenders regularly and take advantage of office hours. The recommenders will have an easy time writing your letter if they can understand your passion, activities, academic achievements, future plans, and motivations. Lastly, make sure to give your recommenders ample time to write your letters. It is encouraged to ask for the letters as soon as possible; however, make sure to give them at least 6-8 weeks in advance.

Important lesson learned with Letter of Recommendations.
I believe that asking and maintaining the letter of recommendations was one of the most stressful factors of my application process. I believe this was because I had no control over writing the letter of recommendations. I had to trust my recommenders that they would follow through and submit their letter in a timely manner. Talking to my friends who were also applying to medical school stated that the letter of recommen-

dation requirement was the most stressful component in their application process – and I will show you why.

I started with the plan of asking 5 people for recommendation letters: 2 science professors, 1 non-science professor, 1 activities adviser, and 1 research mentor. I met them in person in February, and they responded that they would be happy with writing the letter. My research mentor has always been very timely, and was finished with the letter by March. I was extremely grateful for his quick response because now I only needed to worry about 4 other recommenders to get their letter in on time. On March 7th, I decided to submit a reminder email respectfully asking for the letters to be completed by May. I decided to set a tentative deadline for May so I would have enough wiggle time in case the recommenders did not submit the LOR in time. Two of the four recommenders replied to my email and I appreciated the clear communication, especially because I lived 3 hours away from Northwestern and couldn't just knock on their office doors to check on the status (Since I graduated Northwestern in December, I was writing my medical school applications during my gap year).

April rolled by and I decided not to send a reminder email because it was still 1 month away from the May deadline that I had requested. I had waited patiently and was disappointed that the letters were not submitted on May 1st However, since the actual LOR was not due until July, I did not panic. Trying to be responsible, I decided to send a reminder email on May 7th (exactly 2 months after the last reminder email), and also extended the deadline to June 1st. To my despise, I received a pretty frustrated email from one of my science professors asking me to stop sending these reminder emails because they were annoying and inappropriate, and that I "would be better off not sending any more emails." I was incredibly embarrassed, but also confused because I did not think I was being inappropriate considering that I had waited 2 months to send another email. Nevertheless, I sent an apology letter to maintain a good relationship with him.

After I had sent the reminder email in May, I noticed that the only recommender that I had not heard back since February was my "non-science" recommender. Therefore, I attempted to call her and left a voice mail. After a couple of weeks went by, I decided to drive 3 hours and visit Northwestern to try and catch her in her office. Ultimately, I could not get in contact with her and to this day, I do not know what happened with her. On May 30th, I decided not to worry about the non-science letter, and instead I asked one of the physicians I worked with if they were willing to write a letter for me. Thankfully, all of my LOR were in by July 1st which meant that my secondary applications could be processed as soon as I submitted my application.

♠ In order for your secondary application to be reviewed, you must also submit your transcript, LOR, and the Casper Test. Most of the time, most applicants aren't able to have their secondary application reviewed as soon as possible because their LOR weren't in. Therefore, ask your recommenders to submit their letter by July 1st at the latest.

♠ I did not have a non-science recommender which meant that I could not apply to medical schools that required a non-science professors. While about 5-8 medical schools recommended a non-science recommender, only 2-4 medical schools had this as a requirement. Perhaps you can have "back-up" recommenders if you have a strong relationship with many people; however, I was pretty limited with recommenders so I did not have the luxury of having back-up recommenders.

I believe that it is very appropriate to email or meet with your recommenders once a month. This way you can know as soon as possible if one of your recommenders are likely to drop out last minute. I know that one of my recommenders gave me an angry email, but I think I'd rather send reminder emails than have a recommender forget altogether. This actually happened to one of my friends who could not apply this season because her biology professor FORGOT to write her the recommendation letter. Since medical schools do not review the letter of recommendations until your secondary application is submitted, you will be good to go if your recommenders submit their letters by early July.

Do's for letter of recommendation

1. Do get letters from employers, professors, advisers, physicians, and anyone else who is familiar with you and your work ethic
2. Do ask for a letter in person, rather than sending an email. In the case that you live far away, I would send an email asking for a LOR, and also establishing a time to meet in person
3. Provide a resume, transcript, and a draft of the personal statement to her recommender. Also mention specific things you want included in your letter. Most of the time, the writers will actually appreciate the specificity because it makes writing the letter easier. Some may ask you to write a list of adjectives that describes yourself
4. Indicate that you are waiving your right to see the letter. This is something that that is generally recommended
5. Ask in advance (at least 6-8 weeks before the due date). The due date should be July 1st since medical admissions will begin reading the LOR after your secondary application submission.
6. Send a thank you note afterwards

Don't for letter of recommendation

1. Don't choose someone only for their title
Every year, I hear my friends who are ecstatic that the director of XXX would write them a letter of recommendation. Although it would be amazing to receive a letter from someone with high authority, the letter won't be effective if they don't know you well

2. Don't wait until last minute to ask for a letter. Secure letters as soon as possible. It is encouraged to ask in February-March prior to the application cycle. Some professors keep a max number of students that they write every year. It would be unfortunate if they couldn't write you a letter because you asked too late.

CHAPTER 14: INTERVIEWS

Types of Interviews and How to Prepare

There are many different types of interviews that medical schools use such as:

1. **Closed File Individual Interview** – Closed means that the interviewers do not have access to any of your applications materials including grades, MCAT score, resume, letter of recommendations or essays. Interviewers will only know your name and possibly where you are from. Conversations are more likely to occur in this interview format because they ask more open ended questions such "Tell me about yourself," "Why do you want to go to medical school," and "Why do you want to come to our school." Be prepared to answer these generalized interview questions in a clear and succinct way.

2. **Open File Individual Interview** – Open means that the interviewers have access to your entire application. Although this does not mean that all interviewers will actually read your application in full before interviewing you, you should be prepared to answer anything that is included in your application. Be sure to be able to discuss any red flags that may be on your application including any poor grades or legal consequences. Since they have your application, the interview is more likely to be

a more straightforward/question-answer type format. Since there are only 20-30 minutes for the interviewers to get to know you, don't be surprised if they don't make the interview into a conversation.

3. **Partial Open File Interview** – Partial means that interviewers have access to only a limited portion of your application such as your personal statement, secondary essay, Work&Activities essay, and resume. They will most likely not have access to your GPA and MCAT scores.

4. **Multiple Mini Interviews** – MMI is a newer format that is being introduced to more medical schools . MMI is a situational type interview that is very similar to the Casper exam. There may be 8-10 stations consisting of different interview formats. A scenario will be placed outside the door and you will be given 5-8 minutes to answer the question. There are many different types of MMI questions including but not limited to: scenario questions, ethical questions, healthcare questions, personal questions, team-work activities, and acting scenarios. The team-work activity and acting scenario are pretty interesting because it feels different than a traditional interview. In the teamwork station, you will be working together with another student interviewee. The purpose of this task is to showcase your communication and collaboration competencies. In the acting scenario, you will be given a scenario before entering the room. Inside the room is an actor who you will be engaging with.

After I submitted all of my secondary essays in July and early August, I decided to start preparing for interviews by reading books. The first book I bought was Multiple Mini Interview (MMI): Winning Strategies from Admissions Faculty written by Samir Desai back in April 1st to prepare for Casper exams. Since I had already read this book 3-4 months ago when I was preparing for the Casper test, I decided to skim over this book once again.

This was an excellent book to learn about the MMI structure and to practice formulating my answers based on more than 20 practice scenarios.

In mid-August, my two other books finally arrived in the mail. The first book was called "The Medical School Interview: Winning Strategies from Admissions Faculty" written by Rajani Katta and Samir Desai. I decided to read this book first because it was the same author as the MMI book that I read above. I also enjoyed this book because it gave a more general overview of the entire interview process; however, there were a lot of overlap with the MMI book. So if you're on a budget, I would advise you to choose the MMI book over this. The second book was called "The Premed Playbook Guide to the Medical School Interview: Be Prepared, Perform Well, Get Accepted" written by Ryan Gray. I believe this book was comprehensive, phenomenal, and definitely a must buy book! It not only describes how to prepare for interviews, but it also has an extensive list of questions to answer before attending an interview. For example, since I did not have a strong grasp in healthcare type questions, I appreciated that this book had more than 100 questions in insurance questions, policy questions, and ethical questions that I could review. Keep in mind that this book does not give us the answers to those 100 questions. So you will have to put the effort in researching those questions. After completing this book, I felt extremely prepared to answer these concept-based questions.

As I described above, closed-filed Interviews often ask generalized interview questions such as the ones listed in the table below. I originally thought that generating my answers to these generalized interview questions was going to be easy because I had already discussed my personal interests, passion, and beliefs in my personal and secondary essays. However, I quickly recognized that there was a huge difference in my written answer and spoken answer. While my written answers were brief and concise, I noticed that my spoken answers were too long and all over the place. Therefore, I spent the next couple of days writing a brief outline of all the points I wanted to discuss in less than 3 minutes (per interview question).

♠ Below is a list of common generalized interview questions. Before attending the interview, it is imperative that you can answer these questions in under 3 minutes. When you are practicing your answers, I encourage you to write a bullet point list of the important factors that you want to convey. Do not write complete paragraphs when practicing your answers. This will make you sound overly rehearsed and robotic on your interview day.

Tell me about yourself What defines you	Why Medicine? Why specifically osteopathic medicine?	Why do you want to come to our Medical School? What do you have to offer to our Medical School? Why do you think you will be a good fit to our school? ♠ Must research school's website
Tell me about your strengths and weakness	Tell me about a challenge you faced	Diversity type questions

In addition to reading interview prep books, I decided to schedule two mock interviews. Since I bought the Princeton-Review Medical School Counseling which included primary statement, secondary statement, and interview preparation, I took advantage of the 1 hour of mock interview that was included in my package. Since I had my first interview on August 28th at Campbell SOM, I decided to schedule my first mock interview on August 20th.

During my PrincetonReview mock interview, he asked me the usual interview questions and MMI questions. It was a relief that I had a mock interview with him because I noticed how much I blabbered on. I also remember that my "Tell me about Yourself" answer was 7-8 minutes long! This is when the mock interviewer advised me to keep my answers less than 2-3 minutes. I also noticed that I tended to look down whenever I was thinking so we discussed about how we could improve eye contact. From these feedback, I spent some time making my answers more concise and clear.

My second mock interview was with the Northwestern Prehealth office on August 30th. Since first mock interview, I had made some significant revisions so I was curious as to what my advisor would think of my answers. I was asked the usual questions and was excited when my advisor complemented on my answers. She said that I had a good vibe, energy, and enthusiasm that would come across very nicely. The one thing I was criticized on was my verbal tic "you know?." After she mentioned this verbal tic, I began noticing it every single time I used it. For the first time, I had realized how distracting this was. I was appreciative of her comments because this was something I wouldn't have noticed no matter how many times I rehearsed my answers.

♠ Definitely take advantage of every mock interview opportunity you have. Reach out to your undergraduate's prehealth department and ask if they give out mock interviews. Just be aware that there may be certain restrictions such as the number of mock interview you can do. My prehealth department had a requirement that you must be scheduled for at least 1 medical school interview to be able to schedule a mock interview. We were also allowed 1-2 mock interviews at a maximum. In addition, although it may be awkward to do a mock interview with your friends, you should try to find as many friends as you can.

They will notice little verbal tics and other distractions that you don't want to do during an actual medical school interview. On the other hand, make sure you don't over-do it. Practicing too much can make you sound overly rehearsed. The key to not sounding like a robot is to only write down a list of the things you want to talk about, rather than memorizing an entire paragraph of your speech. It will be hard to sound like a robot if you only have a mental outline of the points you want to discuss.

♠ It shouldn't be too hard formulating an outline to the common interview questions. The hardest part of interview preparation will be understanding policy, ethical, and healthcare concepts just because not everyone is up to date on current events. Many interview prepping sites encourage you to be up-to-date on current healthcare policy and what the future direction of healthcare will look like. Always be sure to know the Affordable Care Act (ACA). The topics that I also researched for each school was its state specific abortion and Euthanasia laws.

Interview Strategies

I believe there are some strategies worth speaking to increase your chances of getting an acceptance!

While you should try to submit your MD and DO applications as soon as the application submission opens, you should definitely apply to DO schools as soon as possible. ACCOMAS has different traffic rules than AAMC which means that DO schools can send out interview invitations earlier than MD schools. If your dream is to attend MD schools, then it would be smart to attend a couple of DO interviews to have as much interview practice as you can before your MD interview. Although the specific processes of each interview will be different, I believe that understanding how an interview works will be a huge advantage under your belt. If you make any mistakes or see any weakness from your first interview, then make sure to practice and improve yourself for your future interviews! Furthermore, if you are accepted to that DO school, this shows that your interview went pretty well! Furthermore, receiving an acceptance early on allows you to go into your future interviews with more poise, courage, and confidence!

Disclaimer: Obviously, if you are not going to attend an osteopathic school, do not apply to DO schools for the sole purpose of practicing interviews. This would be an absolute waste of everyone's time and resources.

Another reason to apply at the earliest date is because medical schools most likely use the rolling admissions basis. Make sure to also schedule interviews at the earliest dates because it will increase your chances of getting in and it will also leave room to schedule future interview dates. Most of the time, you will get about 3 possible interview date options. Scheduling the earliest date will give breathing room just in case you get another interview invite in the near future. Unfortunately, if all your dates are filled with interviews and you receive another interview invitation, you will either have to forfeit one interview, or you will have to email admissions stating that you are unavailable for all of the interview dates. In this case, admissions will most likely respond stating that you will be placed back in the interview pool until additional interview openings are made (which are always not guaranteed). Therefore, be smart about how you manage your interview dates. Think about it this way, admissions receive over 5,000 - 15,000 applications per cycle and they offered you an interview invite. If you say that you cannot attend their interview dates, then it just might be easier for them to give that interview slot to someone else who can make it, rather than trying to schedule a time that fits for you. Therefore, accept interview offers as soon as you receive it, and schedule it at the earliest date.

It is possible to be financially smart during your interview season. If you have a school that you are unsure if you would attend and has high travel costs, then it might be smart to schedule it after October 15th. October 15th is the earliest date that MD schools can offer admissions. Therefore, if you happen to receive an admission from a school you like on October 15, then you can start to selectively attend interviews and reject others. Luckily, since I received an acceptance letter on October 15, this allowed me to reject about 4-5 interviews which saved me about $2000 in travel costs.

Other Interview Points

If you were invited for an interview, this means that they are interested in you and that your initial qualifications have already proved that you would be a good candidate for their school – so own your interview! The interview will now be a method to assess your personality and get to you know better personally. They already see your academic performance and are satisfied with it. If you have or had a red flag on your academics, no need to bring this up unless they ask you first. This interview is more to see how well-suited you would be in their environment and values. (I sometimes think that if I get an interview, this means I already have a ticket of entry – I just need to put effort so I won't lose my ticket of entry). There are some additional tips I would like to discuss when attending interviews.

How to Dress
Wear a suit. It should be conservative and clean looking. Although you do not need to press your suit before every interview, it should not have so many wrinkles and folds that it is distracting. Many students will either choose black, navy blue, or charcoal colored suits. If you decide to choose a unique color, make sure the color is not distracting.

Women:
Wear a suit jacket and either a pant/skirt suit. Obviously, the length of the skirt must be appropriate. If you ever question the length of your skirt, or if you constantly see yourself needing

to pull down your skirt to your knees, then change to a longer skirt. If you wear a skirt, panty hose is not required. In fact, I think I've only seen a total of 10 girls during my entire interview season wear panty hose.

Next, consider wearing a scooped top or a loose blouse, rather than collared shirts. Since we do not have ties, most of the collared shirts do not sit well and look crooked. Think what color looks best on you. I've heard not to wear a white top because many people wear white tops and you will just be another herd in the penguin squad.

Consider wearing 1-2.5 inch nude or black heels. Almost all women will wear heels and it just makes you look "dull" if you wear flats. If you do not feel comfortable with heels, then consider wearing 0.5 - 1 inch heels. Also, avoid high heels because they are distracting and you are not going to a club.

Men:
Wear a suit, collared shirt, tie, and dress shoes. I won't spend time elaborating on this because dressing business formal is easy for guys. One piece of advice: wear something your mother will approve.

What to Bring into Interview Rooms
Some schools are very specific in what you can and cannot bring into the interview rooms. Most MMI interviews will not let you take anything into the rooms. Check with what you can bring before the actual interview process starts. I encourage you to bring:

- Water bottle – For some reason, my mouth gets incredibly dry when I start speaking, most likely due to being nervous. It definitely helps to take sips during the interview (of course, at appropriate times) so I don't get "dry mouth."
- Folder or Portfolio – I brought a small portfolio with me to take during interviews. I only brought it during traditional interviews because most MMI interviews did

not allow us to bring portfolios. I never actually opened my portfolio during my interviews, but I brought it for accessory purposes only. I liked how it made me feel professional and prepared.

Questions for interviewers

When the interviewers are done asking you questions, they will give you time for questions. This is a chance for you to ask any questions you may have, as well as to show the interviewers that you are engaged and interested! However, a mistake that many students make is that they ask very specific questions that the interviewers will not know the answer to. Most of the time, the interviewers will not know the entire curriculum or specific programs. Therefore, refrain from asking these specific questions because the interviewers will not know the answer and this will cause an awkward pause in the interview. Instead, ask more open ended questions that the interviewers can answer and engage with! Also make sure to have a list of questions for medical student interviewers and the staff. Throughout my interview, I noticed that I had the most success with the following questions.

To Medical Students:
- Why did you decided to attend XXX? Were there any school specific programs or factors that aided in your decision?
- Any questions about wellbeing: How do students at XXX reduce stress and protect their wellbeing?
- I usually follow-up with anything the student said during the interview. If they speak about a particular program they lead, and you have more interest in that particular program, you should ask about it!

To Physicians, Admissions, Professors, Community Members:
- If you had a daughter (since I am female) who was interested in going to medical school, would you hope that she was interested in attending XXX school? Why?

- Is there a program that exists at XXX that you wish were more highlighted and featured?

♠ Interviewers seemed to like this question because they are most likely going to talk about their program that they are passionate in.

- If I were to poll the students and faculty members about any changes that needs to be made at XXX, what would you predict it to be?

  ♠ Notice how I did not ask "what are the changes that will be made to the curriculum in the future." Most staff do not know the curriculum fully enough to speak about it. Therefore, keep your questions generic and open ended.

Send Thank you Letters within 24 hours

After traditional interviews, it is a good gesture to send thank you letters for your interviewers. Although I have read plenty of posts that these thank you letters do not increase your chances of acceptances, who doesn't like being appreciated? Most interviewers are medical students, professors, physicians, admissions, and community members who are taking time off from their busy schedules to conduct interviews. Therefore, show appreciation for your interviewers by sending thank you letters!

Pay attention to how admissions would like you to send your thank you letters. If appropriate, you can ask the interviewers for their contact information at the end of the interview. Then, you can send a thank you letter directly to the specified email; however, if you either forget to ask for the contact information, or admissions request that you don't ask interviewers for their information, then you can submit your thank you letter to the admissions office. Most of the time, they will be happy to relay that information to the interviewers. In the case that the interview was a MMI interview, you do not have to worry about sending thank you letters.

Here are some helpful tips to keep in mind when drafting your thank you letter

- Send your thank you letter within 24 hours after the interview (email is fine)
- Be respectful. Include their full professional title and name (For professional purposes, I even addressed medical school students by their full name)
- Say thank you and show your appreciation
- Incorporate specific points that occurred in your conversation. Interviewers will interview numerous applicants per day. Therefore, this allows your interviewer to remember who you are!
- One last pitch about yourself! Why do you see that you are a good fit for that school?
- Last remark to show your gratitude
- Closing Line and a professional picture of yourself (so interviewers can really remember who you are)
- Don't expect to receive a response from your interviewers. Just because you did not receive a reply doesn't mean that your interview went poorly. I personally received a response about 60% of the time!

This is a sample thank you letter that I sent to one of my interviewers! (I took out some information because it wasn't too important for the purposes of the book!)

Dear XXX,

My name is Nahee Park and I wanted to thank you for taking the time to meet with me during my interview today at XXX. I was impressed by the friendliness of the faculty members and its community driven curriculum. I believe my personal values of social responsibility resonates with the values of XXX and I am in awe of the immense amount of support given to students to pursue their passions.

It was truly an honor to meet you and I enjoyed discussing about the book XXX and how that narrative was also a part of my family's story. To better understand the XXX, I decided to buy the book through Amazon today! Once again, thank you for giving me the opportunity to share my experiences, skills, and interest. I hope you have a great upcoming weekend!

Sincerely,
Nahee Park
[Picture of myself]

Write Post-interview Reflections After Every Interview

After my interviews, I always wrote post-interview reflections. I described my initial impressions of the faculty, students, and facilities. I made sure to highlight any impressive programs and opportunities of the school along with its strength/weaknesses. I did not want to forget my overall impressions of a school since I knew that the application process was going to be a long one. On an excel spreadsheet, I also color-coded how likely I was going to attend the school if I was accepted (as shown below).

Green	Yes, definitely attend if accepted!
Yellow	There were some weak factors that makes me hesitant
Red	No, will most likely not attend

*Personal thoughts and reflections
on all medical school interviews attended*

Campbell University School of Osteopathic Medicine

Interview Invite	August 7
Interview Date	August 28
Acceptance Notification	August 31

How I prepared for Campbell Interview:
- General Interview questions
- Why DO specifically?
- Why Campbell University SOM?
- North Carolina abortion/euthanasia laws.

After researching Campbell and understanding their mission and goals, I saw that Campbell had an extremely strong emphasis on rural community-based medicine. Since my application focused on identifying community based needs and implementing programs that solved these issues, I was excited to share all of my experiences with the interviewers. Although I wasn't quite sure I was head over heels about practicing in a rural community, living in a medically underserved suburb definitely helped me understand the lack of healthcare access to members in a rural area. This was my very first interview so I didn't exactly know what to expect. But I felt prepared and excited to attend my first interview!

The interview day started at 08:00 so I arrived by 07:45. This was the first interview for the majority of the students so it was fun talking to students and gauging how their application process was going. When I arrived to the interview, there were about 20 interviewees who arrived earlier than me. I was expecting everyone to be talking to each other, but the atmosphere was dead silent. Since this was one of the earliest scheduled interviews, I think we were all just really nervous and unsure how to mingle with each other. It also didn't help that we were all given folders with information because everyone's heads were buried under the folder. However, I decided to put my folder away and started making eye contact to those around me. It seemed that a couple of others were thinking the same thing and as soon as we made eye contact, we began awkwardly introducing ourselves. More and more people began to introduce themselves and this conversation definitely helped ease the tension around.

At 8:00am, the admission director came to the lobby to greet everyone and directed us towards an auditorium to start the day. It started out with the Dean welcoming everyone and giving a 30 minute presentation about all the great things Campbell had to offer. The next thing on the agenda was the interview so everyone was clearly anxious when the presentation was coming to an end.

The interview consisted of three faculty interviews lasting 20 minutes each. Since it was an open file interview, I was ready to answer everything on my application. While some interviewers only asked me basic questions such as "Tell me about yourself," all interviewers asked me "Why Campbell and Why an Osteopathic education." I got a sense that all the interviewers were friendly people who genuinely wanted to get to know me. I showed a lot of enthusiasm and excitement because I was talking about all the organizations/events that I was extremely passionate in. After I answered the "usual generic questions," the rest of the time diverted into a normal natural conversation. Other Events:

- Lunch with CUSOM Students
- Tour of Medical School with CUSOM Students
- Financial Aid Presentation
- Matriculation Documentation
- Wrap Up

Personal Reflections:
Campbell University SOM is in Lillington, North Carolina, a rural town of 3,500 people. No wonder Campbell focused on rural medicine. Although I am not "a city person," I thought this location was too small for me. As a Korean-American, I am looking for a diverse community, and this is something I unfortunately didn't see at Campbell. The facilities were excellent and their technologies were very advanced. I was also inspired by the friendliness of the staff members. The entire interview

went very well and I was ecstatic about the interview. The students seemed very happy about being there. Most of the medical students were originally from rural areas and chose Campbell because of their focus in rural medicine. I was happy that they were fulfilling their passion, but I got a sense of feeling that this was not the best environment for me to be happy in. I recalled that I loved Northwestern's location because it was in Evanston which was close to many Korean churches and restaurants. Although I don't want to live in a city, I thought this rural life was a little too rural for me. Additionally, there were only 2 buildings standing next to each other. Since I was hoping for a "campus feel," I wasn't too excited about how the buildings were isolated from the rest of the community.

Three days later, I received an email that I was accepted! I was happy that I received an acceptance because it was also an indicator that my interview and interview preparation were good enough. This would also allow me to be more confident in my other school interviews. I was very excited that I received my first acceptance. I was even more ready to tackle my future interviews that I was scheduled to attend. Since the deposit fee of $1,500 to hold my seat wasn't due until November, I chose to hold off paying this deposit.

George Washington University School of Medicine

Interview Invite	July 19
Interview Date	September 07
Waitlist Notification	October 17

I was ecstatic that I received an interview from George Washington considering that they select about 1100 students from a pool of 14,000. This was my first MD interview so I was pretty nervous. I had already received an acceptance from Campbell one week before the George Washington interview so I was feeling pretty good. I decided to reserve a hotel right in front of the sch

The interview day started at 09:15 so I arrived there 15 minutes earlier. I checked in with security at 09:00 because I was advised to arrive 10-15 minutes before the start time. When I arrived, there were already 15 applicants who were talking and introducing each other. I walked up, introduced myself, and then held pretty long conversation with 2 girls before we were called into a small room for the interview day to begin.

The interview was open filed with 1 medical school student and a faculty member. I had my first interview with a MD2 student and I thought it went extremely well. There were a total of 20 applicants and the day included informal visits with students, a tour of Ross Hall, diversity presentation, financial aid presentation, and a catered lunch. There were 2 blind interviews: one with a faculty member and one with a current student. The tour itself was unimpressive because the buildings were old and poor (I mean, it's the 11th oldest medical school that was found on 1824). There is one big building called Ross Hall which comprises of 6-7 floors. Renovations were done in 2012 so some floors looked better than others.

PRO:
-In the middle of the city (but perhaps it's too city for me)
-Close to GW undergraduate university. Having a undergrad will mean that there are club and sport activities that I can join.
- Loved how the FoggyBottom station was on the block which means that it is a walking distance to go check out awesome FREE museums and the white house.
- Lots of Korean restaurants, Korean churches. I'm looking for a Korean community so this is definitely on my radar.

- Enjoyed meeting medical students. They were very honest about their stay and all the students seemed that they loved their school. I didn't see too many students "in their natural setting" but they generally seemed happy.
- One thing I loved about GW even before going to the interview was that they had so many opportunities to be involved. They had a program where I could do a 4th year rotation at SNU in Seoul (although now I see that many other medical schools offer international rotations).

CON:

There is only 1 medical facility next to the medical school. I love how some schools have campus feels, so the fact that GW just had 1 building was a con for me. They have no workout room (which doesn't bother me too much.). Since it's the city, I questioned the safety of the community. I asked a lot of students about the safety and they all said that they generally felt safe.
- There are extremely limited student study spaces. Even library which was quite minimal.
- Grading system is Honors, Pass, Conditional, or Fail. I am hoping to attend a school that is pass/fail.

Midwestern University Chicago College of Osteopathic Medicine

Interview Invite	August 26
Interview Date	September 13
Acceptance Notification	September 27

I arrived to Midwestern 15 minutes early and was directed to the "Fish Bowl" room where all the interviewees were waiting for the interview to start. Right off the bat, I was in love with this school based on their campus feel and new facilities. Midwestern had other professional schools (such as Dental, Optometry, Pharmacy, etc) so it immediately felt like a college campus. The facilities were top notch and I was extremely interested in this school's history. I was also extremely impressed by the number of medical students who decided to sneak into the Fish Bowl room to introduce themselves and also ask us if we had any questions about Midwestern. The made the community feel very homey and welcoming.

My interview was an open filed panel with 3 members including faculty members and Ph.D students. Since it was a panel of 3 people, I was intimidated because they constantly threw questions at me; however, I thought I did a good job sharing my story and engaging all three interviewers. It definitely helped that I had many interview practices under my belt to be able to stay confident and speak concisely.

♠ Especially in a panel interview, it is important to engage the interests of all interviewers. My panel consisted of 1 DO physician, 1 biochemistry Ph.D, and 1 MD student. Therefore, I predicted that the DO physician would ask me questions such as "Why medicine, why particularly osteopathic medicine." (In fact, they did). I also assumed that the Ph.D student would be interested in my research opportunities (In fact, they did). Lastly, I assumed that the MD student would ask me any remaining questions such as "Why Midwestern" and take a look into my undergraduate activities (In fact, they did). Since the flow of the questions were how I predicted it, I thought my answers could come out clearly and precisely.

♠ Before the start of interviews, some schools give a list of the interviewer names. If they give you this information, you should spend some time researching who they are before your interview. Since most of my interviews occurred after lunch, I would spend about 5-7 minutes in the bathroom during my lunch break trying to see who my interviewers were and what they did.

Personal Reflection:
I was very impressed by the faculty, buildings, and medical students of this school. I felt that Midwestern had all the qualities that Campbell was lacking such as having diverse group of students. I also appreciated that Midwestern was located in a suburb of Chicago. Since my hometown is only 2-3 hours from Midwestern, I felt very comfortable with the overall location. The only major setback is the tuition of this school which is about $70,000. This means that yearly would be around $90,000 - $100,000 including living expenses. Current medical students said that this was worth it because 100% of the students were accepted to residency. Overall, I thought Midwestern was a great school and I would choose this school over Campbell.

Des Moines University Osteopathic Medical School

Interview Invite	September 12
Interview Date	September 20
Acceptance Notification	October 10

Des Moines University had splendid facilities and the students were extremely friendly. There is nothing more to include other than the interview process. Similarly to the Midwestern interview, the DMU interview was an open filed panel with 3 interviewers including 1 DO physician, 1 professor, and 1 MD student. As soon as I went into the interview, however, I was immediately overwhelmed by the layout of the interview room. There was one chair 30 feet in front of the panel interviewers. The distance between the interviewers and interviewee was way too distant and isolating.

The interviewers introduced themselves and the interview immediately started with an overwhelming amount of questions that were thrown at me. Unlike the Midwestern interview where an interviewer would ask a question which then would transition into a conversation, the interviewers at DMU only asked the question and that was the end of it. As soon as I was done with my answer, the spot light immediately moved on to the next person who would read the next question off of a sheet of paper. Although reading questions off the paper would provide a standard set of questions to be established between the interviewers, it was clearly intimidating because I couldn't personally engage with them. By the end of the interview, I was flushed and noticed that I had sweated through my shirt. I wasn't used to this pressure and knew that the interviewers could tell how nervous I was. Due to this reason, I thought that I did not perform well at all. However, I guess my interview went better than I thought considering that I received an acceptance from this school!

Personal Reflection:
The building was up to date and I appreciated that DMU had a campus. DMU was also a good osteopathic school. However, I was not too big of a fan of the location of where DMU was at. I did not feel a sense of diversity I had felt at Midwestern. I was pretty certain that I would be choosing Midwestern over DMU.

Southern Illinois University School of Medicine

Interview Invite	August 06
Interview Date	September 18
Accept When Place Available (**AWPA**) Notification	November 10
Accepted	April 24

I went to the Dean's Lobby at 08:00 for an interview day that began at 08:15. The interview at SIU was different than all the previous interviews because there were only 3 students other than myself. SIU highlighted how they spent a lot of time giving personalized/individualized attention to students and this was clearly represented through the interview process. I liked the small group because it seemed more friendly, focused, and personalized. After a brief informational session, I had my first interview at 09:00. This interview process was also different because it required that we traveled to their offices. My first interviewer was a faculty who was a professor of surgery. All interviews were open file, so she was scrolling through my application on her computer and asked anything that seemed interesting. I mainly talked about my passion for medicine, why I wanted to come to SIU, and explained the various organizations I was involved at school. I didn't particularly connect with my interviewer but I thought I had answered all of her questions okay.

We had a financial aid presentation, lunch, and a tour. The facility was relatively unimpressive and there were minimal study spaces. There was a pretty large cafeteria that was connected to a hospital and food was alright. I was impressed by the students at SIU because they seemed extremely friendly and open. I appreciated when 15 medical students came to us to say hello and asked us if we had any questions.

The last interview was at 14:00 with another faculty member in the medical education. I really enjoyed interviewing with her and I saw that we clicked instantly. I think our connection started when she said that her son wanted to go to the Illinois Mathematics and Science Academy – which was the high school I graduated from. We also saw that we had a lot in common because I was also really interested in education and providing more academic assistance to underserved students. Therefore, I discussed about the time when I led a team of students in high school presenting an academic bill reform to state senators. She was also very interested in a mentorship program that I was heavily involved with in college. Because this interview felt like a normal conversation, I was surprised when my interview went nearly 1.5 hours! The entire interview was not a "question-answer" process like it was with the first interview, but more of a conversation. At SIU, I had an overall positive influence by the students and faculty; however, the facility was very poor. I also didn't like how the majority, if not all, of the learning system was problem-based learning (PBL). Additionally, SIU is unique because the first year is at Carbondale with the last 3 years being at Springfield. Overall, I came from the interview thinking that I would only attend this school if I didn't have any other MD acceptances.

♠ Problem-Based Learning (PBL) is a curriculum that is implemented in almost all medical schools. While most medical schools incorporate only a small portion of PBL within their curriculum, I noticed that Southern Illinois School of Medicine's main learning curriculum was via PBL. The PBL approach usually includes a case study presentation to a small group of students. The students then understand the problem presented in the case study to learn about the concepts within the problem. More clearly, under the PBL style, students gain knowledge via direct application scenarios (rather than learning the knowledge, then applying it to a real-life scenario). While I believe that knowledge retention is greater under the PBL curriculum, I thought this method would take a longer time to learn. Therefore, I question if this type of learning style is efficient.

Therefore, taking a look at the curriculum style offered at your medical school is important. While the core concept will be the same across all schools, some schools will offer learning styles in a way that you learn best. The two main learning styles will be Problem-Based Learning (Case-based) and Lecture-based learning. I believe that I learn best when I first understand concepts through a lecture-based style, then confirm and apply my knowledge through the PBL style.

Medical College of Wisconsin (MCW)

Interview Invite	August 28
Interview Date	September 28
Acceptance notification	October 15

I was immediately impressed by the facilities of MCW as soon as I walked inside the building. MCW was unique because they offered a social event the night before the interview which would serve as an opportunity for applicants to meet with current MCW MD students. From the student panel and the friendliness of the students, I was already looking at this school from a positive light. There was a student hosting program at MCW, but I chose to sleep in a hotel because I wanted as much as rest I could get.

The morning started off with the usual introduction, curriculum introduction, and MCW spotlight presentations. The interview was 2 open filed individual interviews with 1 faculty and 1 student. MCW had a strong emphasis in community driven curriculum and a dedication to serve the community. I believed that my accomplishments and passions were clearly aligned with the mission of this school. Therefore, I felt like I could be myself and do well by just sharing my stories. I believed that both my interviews went well!

MCW used to have a 5-point grading system, but they said that they would change to pass/fail by 2019 cycle. I was very happy with this change. I enjoyed talking with all the students and I could clearly see why MCW accepted them in the first place. For the first time, I could see myself at MCW and thought that my views and passions in life were similar to the other students I had met. I remember coming out of the interview very happy and confident that I had found a school that I felt belonged to.

I was excited to receive an acceptance letter on October 15th - the first possible date to be accepted by an allopathic medical school.

♠ Listen to your initial instincts about a school. I remember that I came out having a good feeling about this school and saying to myself "Wow, I could really see myself in this school." I'm glad that my interviewers and admission officers saw me in the same way!

Albany Medical College

Interview Invite	August 27
Interview Date	October 03
Waitlist Notification	November 26
Accepted from Waitlist	January 23
Withdraw my application	January 24

When my plane first landed in Albany, I was very hesitant with the location of the school. Although many people say that geographical location shouldn't be the end all be all (I mean, of course it can't be your sole decision), I believe that your first instincts of a location should be factored in. If you're unhappy in an area, it's most likely going to be difficult changing that mindset as a student.

Despite my initial impression of the school, I still was excited to attend another MD school interview. Going down the hotel elevator to walk to the medical school (I chose a hotel that was right in front of the medical school), I met another applicant that would end up being my buddy throughout the day! Walking into the school, I thought the facilities were not only poor, but almost creepy. During the lunch student panel, I saw that the current medical students seemed tired, exhausted, and worn out. They didn't seem to like their school and this showed from their lack of enthusiasm for the school. Although I kept in mind that these student ambassadors were only a small cohort of the entire student population, I remember thinking that I wanted to attend a medical school where students loved their school. When I hear comments such as, "there's nothing to do around here, but that doesn't matter because all you will be doing is studying and you will never leave this building," I back out a little. Yes, of course medical school will be difficult, but I am hoping to attend a medical school where I can be involved with the community and enjoy myself. I would especially like to have the option of choosing not to leave the medical building – rather than not being able to leave the building cause there is nothing else out there.

This school was my first MMI interview format and wasn't quite sure what it would be like. I reviewed all my MMI materials 1-2 days before the interview. I unfortunately can't give out more details of my MMI interview because I signed a waiver; however, I believe that the MMI interview went "okay." I was glad that I spent time reading MMI books and searching up some MMI videos on Youtube because they were very representative of the actual MMI interview.

After my interview was over, I decided that this medical school was not for me. Therefore, I wasn't too anxious of the decision. I ended up getting waitlisted on November 26th, which was exactly where I thought I would be. I was then accepted from the waitlist on January 23rd. However, since I had acceptances from University of Minnesota and Medical College of Wisconsin that I loved, I decided to withdraw my application on January 24th to give the seat to someone else who deserved it! To be considerate of other applicants, I should have withdrawn my application from Albany as soon as I received acceptances from other schools.

University of Colorado School of Medicine

Interview Invite	August 29
Interview Date	October 05
Waitlist Notification	November 27

I landed in Denver, Colorado and absolutely loved the atmosphere. It was a new feeling because it was busy like the city, but I didn't feel suffocated. I remember looking from the balcony of my hotel overlooking Denver and I just thinking, "Wow, what a beautiful scenery."

The UColorado interview was drastically different and more exhausting than all the other interviews I attended. It consisted of a team work activity, group interview, and an individual interview. There were over 60 interviewee applicants sitting together in an auditorium, so it was certainly the largest interview session I ever went too! Despite the large number of applicants, they did an incredible job of organizing the interview because all the events occurred very smoothly and quickly.

We first had a team work activity which consisted groups of three doing a team building exercise. There were two faculty members observing us and writing feedback on our communication/team-working skills. I had so much fun working with my teammates during the team work activity. I thought I did a good job leading discussions and also giving time for other group members to speak their opinions. I saw that everyone enjoyed this team building exercise and we definitely had more fun than we were supposed too! I even forgot that I was being evaluated.

The second evaluation was a group interview. We were separated into different groups of three, and I would say this was the more "intimidating" evaluation of the entire interview. We were sitting in front of two interviewers who asked numerous situational questions. The hardest task was to balance leading discussions but also making sure to listen to others and give an answer that has not been mentioned. I remember there was an applicant who was more "dominant" and wanted to lead every discussion. On the other hand, there was another applicant who was the "quiet" one. I saw this as an opportunity to be the "balancer" by leading questions while also providing an opportunity for the "quiet" girl to speak as well.

♠ The most important thing during a group interview is knowing when to lead and when to back off. Leading all discussions can seem that you don't care about collaboration. However, being too quiet also seems like you are not confident and don't have anything to add to the discussion. An interesting observation I made was that I didn't have any male applicants in my group. I sometimes wonder how the dynamic could have changed if there was a male applicant.

The last event was an individual interview with a panel of 2 faculty members. Similar to Des Moines University's (DMU) process, the interviewers had a piece of paper with a list of questions to choose from. This was more of a question-answer type interview which made it difficult to engage what the interviewers were thinking about me.

Overall, I thought I did pretty well with the interviews. I felt that I was somewhat nervous with my individual interview so I'm not sure if this was something that the interviewers saw as well. I loved the school and I loved the campus feel that U Colorado had. The library was incredible, and there was a children's hospital that was exceptional. Being a Disney fan, I loved that the children's hospital was designed by Disney! I instantly fell in love with this school and I believe that it became my first choice. I loved the surrounding community and thought that I would do well and be happy here.

The interviews were tough and there were many applicants

who were equally as qualified. The only downside to this school is that the OOS tuition is incredibly high at about $62,000. I ended up being waitlisted and was pretty bummed about the result. However, I am hoping to get off the waitlist!

On April 23rd, I received an email that I had been placed on the "top priority category" of the waitlist. This meant that my position was in the top one-third of the alternate list. The email also indicated that there was a high probability that I would receive an acceptance offer. Historically, almost all top-tier waitlist students were accepted; therefore, I was pretty confident that I would too get accepted. However, unfortunate as it is, I ultimately did not receive an acceptance letter.

Western Michigan University Homer Stryker MD School of Medicine

Phone Interview Invite	August 08
Phone Interview Date	August 20
Campus Interview Invite	September 05
Campus Interview Date	October 12
Waitlist Notification	October 29

Western Michigan had a unique application process because it had a phone interview prior to giving a campus interview. I was incredibly happy to receive a phone interview on August 20th. I was pretty nervous since this was my first interview. Again, due to a confidentiality commitment, I cannot release specific information about the interview. The phone interview was also interesting because it was handled by a third company. This meant that they most likely did not have access to my application. I believe that the purpose of the third company was to access our personality. After the phone interview was over, I have to say that I was extremely bummed because I thought I bombed it. I completely froze and panicked because I could not think of an answer to one of the questions.

♠ During an interview, if you are asked a question that completely throws you off, do not panic. Instead, ask them for some time to think about your answer. This is better than blabbering, or stating something that you do not mean.

To my surprise, I received an on campus interview invite! Some posts from SDN (student doctor network) mentioned that about 50% of the phone interview turns into a campus interview, so I guess I did well enough to be in that 50%! My interview at Western Michigan was "meh." This is a new medical school with its first graduating class being this year. I definitely was cautious knowing that this was an extremely new medical school. Since it is a new school, the facilities were impressive! Western Michigan had a HUGE simulation floor! Nearly all medical schools have some kind of simulation lab/room; however, Western Michigan had an entire floor of simulation equipment. Another interesting feature of this school is that the USMLE Step 1 is taken during their 3rd year. They said that students often do better on the step exam after doing some clinicals; however, I think I would want to take it at the end of my 2nd year to get it out of the way.

The interview consisted of an open filed interview along with a situational type interview. Due to signing a waiver, I will keep it at that! Despite the high average stats of Western Michigan, I was pretty certain that I would not attend this school, unless this was the only school I was admitted to. The surrounding community seemed reassuring; however, I didn't feel that this school would be for me.

Warren Alpert Medical School of Brown University

Interview Invite	September 24
Interview Date	October 25
Waitlist Notification	November 19

I was excited for this interview because it was Brown!! - and because it was my first time going to Rhode Island. My interview day starting with all the interviewees getting together and immediately getting to know each other - I would say that this was the most fun group of interviewees. However, this interview seemed like it was the most disorganized. Admissions said that the original room was being occupied with a meeting so we went to another room that didn't have a screen. Without a PowerPoint presentation, I felt that the admissions officers did not do a good job highlighting all the cool programs Brown had to offer. I remember precisely thinking that Brown had so many awesome programs and curriculum; however, admissions didn't talk about any of those unique programs/pathways. If I had not done my research before coming to the Interview, I probably would have left the interview without knowing anything about Brown.

The interview consisted of 2 open filed individual faculty interviewers. My first interview was with a faculty member and honestly, I do not know why I did so poorly with it. I was not nervous, but I think it's because I was overly excited. My interviewer asked me questions that I had already answered numerous times in the past such as "Tell me about yourself, Why medicine, Tell me about your research, etc." However, I was not clear with my answers and I blabbered through most of my answers. To tell you precisely, I remember she asked me about my most RECENT research project. Rather than diving in to my most recent research project, I started telling my entire life story and how I started doing research since high school. I saw my interviewer getting bored and that was the worst feeling ever. My interview with her was done and I just left the room thinking that if I was the interviewer interviewing someone like me, I would be equally as bored.

So I knew I had to do better with my 2nd interviewer who was the director of the Emergency Department. I walked into my 2nd interviewer knowing the changes I had to make, but at the same time, I needed to forgot how badly I had just performed with my 1st interviewer. He asked me similar questions such as "Tell me about yourself, Why Medicine, etc." I made sure to state only the important points and state it clearly. I forgot the details of this interview, but I remember that I decided to discuss a book (The Power of Habits) I had read and how it positively changed my outlook in life. I remember that he was in awe of my new ideology and he said that my answer had "blew his mind." He seemed to be very interested in me and I was so relieved that I had made a good impression on him.

In the end, I received the waitlist email and I was pretty bummed about this; however, I was expecting this result because I knew how poorly I performed with my 1st interviewer. Overall, although I wasn't too impressed from my interview at Brown, I liked the programs that Brown had to offer from their website. I also loved Providence and how the Brown undergraduate was fairly close to the medical school. Ultimately, I received an email in June that they were no longer accepting students.

University of Minnesota School of Medicine

Interview Invite	October 31
Interview Date	November 13
Acceptance Call	December 19
Acceptance Email	January 2

I was extremely surprised to receive an interview invitation from University of Minnesota just because they rarely take Out of state (OOS) applicants. I originally decided to apply to U of Minnesota because my brother was doing a Ph.D. program at the time. I definitely talked about this in my application when they asked if I had any ties to University of Minnesota.

I arrived to Minnesota a couple of days before my interview so I could visit my brother. I remember how deadly the weather was because it was about 10F with windchills. Honestly, I went to the interview not putting too much significance to it. They did the usual welcoming presentation and curriculum introductions. The interview was a MMI style. I was glad that I had a MMI experience from Albany medical college. The MMI consisted of partner exercises and an acting scenario. I remember that the acting scenario was intense because the discussion/situation was based on a controversial topic. Honestly, I went through each of the MMI rooms thinking that I would do my best – but at the same time, I didn't worry too much about each of the MMI because I thought I liked MCW better at the time.

At the end of the interview, my brother came to pick me up and asked how I did. I remember that my response was "I don't know, I don't care, I probably didn't get in." In the end, I was extremely surprised that I was accepted! After some reflection, I believe that my neutral perspective about the interview allowed me to be comfortable, relaxed, and confident. I remember that I was sometimes too nervous or too excited that I didn't do well as much as I could because I had a lot of energy and thought going through me. For example, when I went to Brown for an interview, I was extremely excited and could not formulate my answers as well as I could have. Therefore, I believe that I was able to be calm, yet still enthusiastic, to be able to deliver my genuine and articulate self to the Minnesota admissions officers. They probably thought that I was very composed who was able to articulate ideas very concisely and clearly.

♠ Having an acceptance helps because it allows you to be more calm about the entire application process. Being nervous, frantic, and placing too much pressure on yourself makes it impossible to articulate yourself. I saw this happen to me during my U Colorado interview and Brown. I remember that I wanted the acceptance so badly that I was too antsy. Knowing how easily I was able to deliver myself to University of Minnesota, I advise you to take some pressure off yourself before going to interviews. At the same time, it is definitely not appropriate to be apathetic or negative! I was still extremely excited to receive an interview invite!

Interviews Declined

I received interviews from Rocky Vista, Rosalind Franklin, Oakland, UMKC, Loyola, Penn State, and University of Illinois but decided to withdraw my application from these schools. There are a couple of schools that were easy to immediately withdraw because I had received an acceptance from a school I liked better. Some of these schools, I actually chose an interview date then decided not to attend.

The most surprising interview that I declined was University of Illinois (UIC). I had been an Illinois resident for 22 years and was expecting a UIC interview pretty early in the cycle. After a long wait, I finally received the UIC interview invite on February 12th and scheduled my interview date on February 22nd. Since I am from Peoria, and there is a UIC Peoria campus, the admissions allowed me to interview in Peoria. However, after some research and calling the admissions officer, I realized that the UIC Chicago campus seats were pretty much filled and they were looking for students for their two other campuses: Peoria and Rockford, Illinois. Since I was already accepted to University of Minnesota and Medical College of Wisconsin, I thought to myself that I would only consider attending UIC if I was accepted at the Chicago campus, or if I was given tuition scholarships. Since the UIC instate tuition was pretty similar to the out of state tuition for University of Minnesota, I knew that my in-state tuition benefit was not significant enough sway me to UIC. Also, only 5-6 Illinois students can get full or partial tuition scholarships. Since I was confident that I would attend University of Minnesota over University of Illinois, I decided to withdraw my application. I am hoping that a student who has not received an acceptance will be able to take my interview spot! Below is the type of email I sent to each of the schools that I declined.

Dear XXX Admissions,

I am very grateful and honored to have received an interview invitation. Thank you for taking the time to review my application and considering me as a candidate. Unfortunately, due to a change of plans, I will not be able to attend the interview. With respect, I would like to withdraw my application at this time. I apologize that I could not be prompt with my decision.

Thank you,
XXX (AAMC: ########)

♠ Although you could be automatically withdrawn from a school if you don't schedule an interview within a specific time period, I think it is pertinent to maintain a good relationship with all schools by sending a short, but genuine email. After sending the email asking to be withdrawn, I always received an email from admissions thanking me for my email and confirming my withdrawal. This email is also creates an opportunity for other students to receive an interview invite in a timely manner. I think this behavior is healthy for all parties involved.

CHAPTER 15: POST INTERVIEW TIPS

Acceptance Letter

First of all, congrats on your acceptance letter! You have come a long way to get this far and I am extremely excited for you! Now, the hardest part is done, but there are still a few things to keep in mind after you get your acceptance letter! Here are a few tips for you:

1. Never turn down an acceptance without the assurance that you are accepted somewhere else. I had a friend who was accepted to a DO school, but turned this down because he thought he would get off at the waitlist from a couple MD schools. In the end, he did not receive any acceptances which caused him to reapply the following year. Therefore, pay the deposit and hold your seat until you know you gained an acceptance from somewhere else.

2. If you have multiple acceptances, and you know a school that you will be declining, do so as soon as possible. Give a chance for someone else to have the joy of an acceptance!

3. Respond to acceptance letters immediately because most schools have a 2 week deadline before a deposit is due. If you miss the payment deadline, then your acceptance will be automatically withdrawn. Thet deposit are

usually $100-200 for MD schools, and $500-2000 for DO schools. While some MD schools will refund this deposit if you decide not to attend, most MD and all of DO school will not return your money. It beats me why DO schools require a higher deposit fee compared to MD schools.

Waitlist Letter

In many ways, getting waitlisted is more painful because it adds to the uncertainty than being straight-up rejected. If you already have an acceptance, then this will relieve some stress. Even if you have no acceptances, you still have hope because many students get off from the waitlist every year. In order to maximize your chances of getting off the waitlist, there are a couple of more things to do to your application. Therefore, spring into action!

1. Write a 1 page letter of interest that includes how your unique talents, characters, attributes align with the schools' mission. Include any new updates or experiences you have done since your application. This letter should describe why you would be a good candidate for the particular school. Make sure to know if schools are receptive to updates. Some schools are very clear that they don't receive updates or letter of interest (such as University of Colorado Medical School). Some schools only take significant updates such as GPA, publications, or MCAT scores. It would be a waste of time to draft a well-written statement only to find out that the school is not receptive to updates.

2. Gain an extra letter of reference from an activity that you started, or from someone who didn't write a letter of recommendation in your initial application.

3. Write 1 letter of intent to a school that is your dream school. Although it is non-binding, this letter serves as a purpose to relay to the school that if you are accepted,

then you are ready to commit. It is advised that you don't play this around. Meaning, do not send letter of intents to multiple schools. I'm sure different medical admissions committees know each-other, and although it would be rare, it would not be in your favor if they found out that you submitted a letter of intent to multiple schools.

4. Be ready to be flexible to accept an offer even in August. I know many people who were called right before orientation began.

This being said, do not bombard schools with numerous updates or letters. It is imperative that you only send 1-2 updates during the entire process, or send only significant updates. Overdoing updates or constantly spamming admissions will put you at a worse spotlight.

Rejection Letter

Rejection isn't easy to handle especially considering all the hard work you put in. Nevertheless, medical school acceptance is lower than 50% so know that you are definitely not alone. There are many qualified applicants and only a limited number of spots.

Short-term Rectification

Make an appointment with your premed/prehealth advisor. Discuss what went wrong and if you should reapply. If you are truly committed to going to medical school, then your decision of reapplying is straightforward. Since as much as 1/3 of medical school applicants are students who are reapplying, do not feel bad about yourself. According to AAMC, there were a total of 52,777 applicants for the Fall 2018 entering class. Out of 52,777 applicants, 73% were first-time applicants and 27% were re-applicants[26]. Unfortunately, there is no data that differentiates how many re-applicants were applying a second, third, or fourth time.

Ask your premed advisor to give an honest constructive feedback on your application. They will be able to see your application and help strengthen your application. Your adviser will most likely have a discussion about all the important factors involved in a holistic review. Furthermore, some medical schools will provide feedback after the application cycle is over. Therefore, contact medical schools that rejected you and politely request if they are willing to meet or do a phone call to discuss how you can improve your candidacy. Since only 50% of applicants are accepted, most medical schools will be familiar with these requests and will be happy to help you.

Before you set up a meeting, I encourage you to take a look at your application and think of some factors where you think you could improve on. Admissions will appreciate your self-reflection. Here are some of the factors that you should think about to improve your application.

Weakness	How to Improve
Poor GPA/MCAT	Retake the classes to rectify individual grades, or take a Post-Bacc Program Retake MCAT
Lack of Community Service	Join an organization you are passionate about, and volunteer regularly
Lack of Clinical Experiences	Shadow physicians, Volunteer at a hospital, work as a medical scribe, EMT, or technician
Lack of Research	Be involved in a research project!
Poor Application	Perhaps you decided to put

> together an application with-
> out spending an adequate
> amount of time. Even though
> your resume may be great,
> perhaps your essays didn't re-
> flect who you were, why you
> want to pursue medicine, or
> your level of maturity

When applying again, rewrite your essay. Every school will keep a record of your old application. Show the changes that you made between your 1st application and 2nd application. It is crucial to see how you have improved in your confidence, maturity, enthusiasm, etc.

You may also decide not to apply again. Perhaps you have went through the maximum number of times you can apply. Perhaps your passion in medicine is no longer there, or you discovered a different path to take. Whatever the reason may be, pursuing a different path in life is completely appropriate. There is no shame in your decision. I give you the best of luck!

CHAPTER 16: BOOKS TO READ

Below is a list of books I bought throughout my medical school journey. The first category of books are those that I read just for fun. Nonetheless, I believe that these books gave me a much larger understanding and breath in medicine. The knowledge and perspective I gained from these books have most likely assisted me during my medical school interviews. The other two categories are books that I thought directly aided me during my medical school application journey. I encourage you to look up these books and go through which ones would help you most during your application journey. Please keep in mind that some of these books were written a very long time ago, and there may be more recent editions available. Enjoy!

Just for Fun Books
- Gifted Hands: The Ben Carson Story by Ben Caron
- The Man Who Mistook His Wife for a Hat by Oliver Sacks
- Being Mortal: Medicine and What Matters in the End by Atul Gawande
- Better by Atul Gawande
- The Checklist Manifesto by Atul Gawande
- When Breath Becomes Air by Paul Kalanithi
- The Immortal Life of Henrietta Lacks by Rebecca Skloot
- The Power of Habit by Charles Duhigg
- The Power of Now: A Guide to Spiritual Enlightenment by Eckhart Tolle

Application Process Preparation

- Med School Confidential by Robert H. Miller and Daniel M Bissell
- The Medical School Admissions Guide: A Harvard MD's Week-by-Week Admissions Handbook by Suzanne M. Miller
- Medical School Essays That Made A Difference (4th & 5th Edition) by Princeton Review
- The MedEdits Guide to Medical School Admissions: Practical Advice for Applicants and Their Parents
- MCAT 2015 What the Test Change Means for you Now by Kaplan
- Getting Into Medical School by Baron's
- Ultimate Guide to Medical Schools by U.S. News
- The BEST 167 Medical Schools (2016) by Princeton Review
- MSAR Subscription

Interview Preparation

- The Premed Playbook: Guide to the Medical School Interview, by Ryan Gray (MUST GET!)
- The Medical School Interview: Winning Strategies from Admissions Faculty by Rajani Katta and Samir P Desai
- Multiple Mini Interview (MMI): Winning Strategies from Admissions Faculty

CHAPTER 17: FINAL WORDS

Congratulations for reaching the end of this book! I hope my story of a successful application process was able to give you insider tips and tools to guide you throughout your pre-med journey. Remember, while GPA and MCAT scores are very important, these are not the only factors that goes into an applicant's candidacy. There are so much more that the student can do in order to have a successful application journey, an important fact for students who don't have stellar MCAT and GPA scores. Since medical school admissions perform a holistic review of an applicant, even the student's non-academic traits such as cultural competency, communication skills, and interpersonal skills will also be reviewed.

During my undergraduate years at Northwestern, I was terrified that I wouldn't be accepted to medical school because I witnessed my friends and peers getting rejected despite their 3.9+ GPA and 520+ MCAT scores. Since I knew that it was virtually impossible for me to obtain these stats, I was immediately devastated and began formulating my Plan B just in case I was rejected too. However, I soon began to realize that most of these students locked themselves in their rooms and studied all day to maintain their stellar scores. This prevented them from joining extra-curricular activities, serving in underserved communities, volunteering in hospitals, and most of all, building interpersonal relationships with people. Therefore, even though their academic achievements were phenomenal and definitely something to be envious of, their absence in participation and engagement resulted in them writing a poor personal statement. In the end, I believe that they were rejected because they could not convince medical school admissions why they were interested in medicine and how they confirmed their passion due to their lack of experiences.

My life motto is "Balance is Key." It truly is. Unless you are a superhuman, I think it's virtually impossible to obtain perfect GPA and MCAT scores, while also researching, serving in a community, starting a new club, attending medical mission trips, becoming a teaching-assistant, playing sports, attending church, and spending time with friends and family. It's all way too much. Therefore, get to know yourself and your limits. See where you can invest time and prioritize. Know how to balance yourself with what you've got.

Overall, I hope that I was able to convince you that you can have a successful application process even if you feel like you are an average student. The medical application process is an exceptionally long journey and I bet you've been riding your pre-med train for quite some time. However, I can assure you that when you receive an acceptance letter, you will forget all the long nights and stressful days of being a pre-med student. I am incredibly grateful for my friends and family who have supported me all this way. I am finding myself getting off this premed train stop and transferring to the medical school train. I hope your premed train ride has been stable and I look forward to the day when we can ride together as physicians.

ABOUT THE AUTHOR

Nahee Park (BA, MD Candidate) graduated high school from Illinois Mathematics and Science Academy in 2014, and received a BA in neuroscience from Northwestern University on December 2017. At Northwestern, Nahee found great meaning and joy in mentoring students. She became the president of the Illuminate Mentorship Program, which provided standardized tests and college application counseling to underserved high school students. Nahee was the recipient of the KSEA Scholarship and Korean Honor Scholarship for her demonstration of high academic achievement, leadership, and community service. During her gap year, Nahee became a full-time emergency department medical scribe while volunteering in the Peoria Rescue Ministries as a computer educator. She also continued her passion by tutoring students in standardized tests, in addition to writing this book in order to guide undergraduate premed students towards a smoother and more successful medical school application process. Nahee will be attending Medical College of Wisconsin in the fall of 2019.

REFERENCES

1. Northwestern University HPA. Applying to Medical School. (n.d.), [Advising Handout]. Health Professions Advising, Northwestern University, Evanston, IL.

2. Northwestern University HPA. Required Courses. (n.d.), www.northwestern.edu/health-professions-advising/pre-med/required-courses/index.html (accessed December 11, 2018)

3. AAMC Table A-17: MCAT and GPAs for Applicants and Matriculants to U.S. Medical Schools by Primary Undergraduate Major, 2018-2019, (2018), www.aamc.org/download/321496/data/factstablea17.pdf (accessed February 16, 2019)

4. Shemmassian Academic Consulting. MD vs DO Admissions: What are the Differences? (n.d.), www.shemmassianconsulting.com/blog/md-vs-do-admissions-what-are-the-differences (accessed January 12, 2019)

5. AAMC Table A-16: MCAT Scores and GPAs for Applicants and Matriculants to U.S. Medical Schools, 2017-2018 through 2018-2019, (2018), www.aamc.org/download/321494/data/factstablea16.pdf (accessed February 22, 2019)

6. AAMC Table A-23: MCAT and GPA Grid for Applicants and Acceptees to US. Medical Schools, 2017-2018 through 2018-2019 (aggregated), www.aamc.org/download/321508/data/factstablea23.pdf (accessed February 22, 2019)

7. AACOM. General Admission Requirements. (n.d.), www.aacom.org/become-a-doctor/applying/general-admission-requirements (accessed February 22, 2019)

8. AACOM. AACOMAS Applicant Pool Profile Entering Class 2018, 2018, www.aacom.org/docs/default-source/data-and-trends/2018-aacomas-applicant-pool-profile-summary-report.pdf?sfvrsn=2ced2197_4 (accessed February 22, 2019)

9. Shemmassian Academic Consulting. What MCAT Score Do You Need to Get Into Medical School? (n.d.), www.shemmassianconsulting.com/blog/mcat/

#part-4-where-to-apply-to-medical-school= (accessed January 23, 2019)

10. AAMC. MCAT Scheduling Fees. (n.d.), https://students-residents.aamc.org/applying-medical-school/article/2015-mcat-registration-fees/ (accessed January 15, 2019)

11. AAMC. The MCAT® Essentials for Testing Year 2019. 2019, pp. 16. https://aamc-orange.global.ssl.fastly.net/production/media/filer_public/66/4c/664c14ab-f87e-435a-82ff-d112a89cc3f9/essentials_2019_-final_10262018.pdf (accessed February 24, 2019)

12. AAMC. Summary of MCAT Total and Section Scores. (n.d.), https://aamc-orange.global.ssl.fastly.net/production/media/filer_public/2c/76/2c767bca-4020-45d6-beb6-7b3bcd3baff6/mcat_total_and_section_score_percentile_ranks_2018_for_web.pdf (accessed February 24, 2019)

13. CASPer. Schools and Programs. (n.d.), https://takecasper.com/schools-and-programs/ (accessed January 20, 2019)

14. AAMC. Table A-24: MCAT and GPA Grid for Applicants and Acceptees by Selected Race and Ethnicity, 2013-2014 through 2015-2016 (Aggregated). (2015), https://www.aamc.org/data/facts/applicantmatriculant/157998/factstablea24.html (accessed March 20, 2019)

15. AAMC. Table A-12: Applicants, First-Time Applicants, Acceptees, and Matriculants to U.S. Medical Schools by Race/Ethnicity, 2015-2016 through 2018-2019. (2018), https://www.aamc.org/download/321480/data/factstablea12.pdf (accessed March 20, 2019)

16. AAMC. Table-18: MCAT Scores and GPAs for Applicants and Matriculants to U.S. Medical Schools by Race/Ethnicity, 2018-2019. (2018), https://www.aamc.org/download/321498/data/factstablea18.pdf (accessed March 20, 2019)

17. AAMC. Table A-2.4: Undergraduate Institutions Supplying 50 or More Asian Applicants to U.S. Medical Schools, 2018-2019. (2018), https://www.aamc.org/download/321456/data/factstablea2-4.pdf (accessed March 20, 2019)

18. AAMC. What are the Benefits of the Fee Assistance Program. (n.d.), https://students-residents.aamc.org/applying-medical-school/article/what-are-benefits-fee-assistance-program/ (accessed March 20, 2019)

19. AAMC. Fact or Fiction: Reviewing Data from the Official Guide to Medical School Admissions. (n.d.), https://students-residents.aamc.org/advisors/article/fact-or-fiction-reviewing-data-official-guide-medi/ (accessed March 20, 2019)

20. Northwestern University HPA. Gap Year. (n.d.), www.northwestern.edu/health-professions-advising/pre-med/gap-year.html (accessed March

20, 2019)

21. Northwestern University HPA. Writing a Personal Statement. (n.d.), [Advising Handout]. Health Professions Advising, Northwestern University, Evanston, IL.

22. Northwestern University HPA. AMCAS Work and Activities/Common Secondary Prompts. (n.d.), [Advising Handout]. Health Professions Advising, Northwestern University, Evanston, IL.

23. AACOM. Experiences. (n.d.), https://help.liaisonedu.com/AACOMAS_Applicant_Help_Center/Filling_Out_Your_AACOMAS_Application/Supporting_Information/2_Experiences (accessed March 23, 2019)

24. AACOM. Achievements. (n.d.), https://help.liaisonedu.com/AACOMAS_Applicant_Help_Center/Filling_Out_Your_AACOMAS_Application/Supporting_Information/3_Achievements (accessed March 23, 2019)

25. Passport Admissions. Medical School Secondary Prompts. (n.d.), http://www.passportadmissions.com/students/medical-schools-by-state/ (accessed March 2, 2019)

26. AAMC. Table A-7.2: Applicants, First-Time Applicants, Acceptees, and Matriculants to U.S. Medical Schools by Sex, 2009-2010 through 2018-2019. (2018), https://www.aamc.org/download/492954/data/factstablea7_2.pdf (accessed March 14, 2019)